FARMHOUSE
FIDDLERS

Music & Dance Traditions in the Rural Midwest

"The Big Four."

FARMHOUSE FIDDLERS

Music & Dance Traditions in the Rural Midwest

by Philip Martin

Photographs Edited by Lewis Koch

Midwest Traditions, Inc.
Mount Horeb, Wisconsin
1994

Leonard Finseth, at home.

Midwest Traditions, Inc. is a nonprofit educational organization devoted to the study and preservation of the folk arts and traditional cultures of the American Midwest. Our publications serve to bring this rich, diverse heritage to broader public attention.

For a catalog of books and other materials, write:

Midwest Traditions
P.O. Box 320
Mount Horeb, WI 53572

(or call toll-free 1-800-736-9189)

Special thanks to the Wisconsin Arts Board, State of Wisconsin, and to the Friends of Midwest Traditions for support to help establish this publishing effort.

© 1994 Philip Martin

ISBN 1-883953-06-5
Library of Congress Catalog Card #94-78042

Manufactured in the United States of America
Printed on acid-free paper
This is printing number: 10 9 8 7 6 5 4 3 2 1

Book Design: Lisa Teach-Swaziek, PeachTree Design
Editor: Jean Johnson

Publisher's Cataloging in Publication
Martin, Philip, 1953-
Farmhouse fiddlers : music & dance traditions in the rural Midwest / by Philip Martin ; photographs edited by Lewis Koch.
p. cm.
Includes bibliographical references.
ISBN 1-883953-06-5

1. Folk music–Middle West–History and criticism. 2. Fiddlers–Middle West. 3. Dancing–Middle West–History. 4. Country life–Middle West. 5. Middle West–Social life and customs.   I. Title.

ML3561.F5M37 1994   781.62'00977
                                               QBI94-1491

Photographs

Photographs by Lewis Koch are protected by copyright and reproduced courtesy of the artist; any unauthorized reproduction is prohibited.

Many photos in this book are made from copies borrowed from private family collections; the kind support of family members for this historical documentation of traditional old-time music is thankfully recognized.

The rest of the images came from public archives. The primary source was the State Historical Society of Wisconsin, whose photographic collections are among the finest in the nation. Their outstanding assistance for this project is greatly appreciated. Other images used in the research and preparation of this book came from ethnic, county, and local museums and historical associations. Their commitment to preserving our diverse cultural legacy is commended.

More complete information on photographs is given in Appendix: Photographic Credits.

Featured on Front Cover: Selmer Oren fiddling (from photo by Lewis Koch, p. 122). Front Cover, Inset (upper): Young musicians on porch (courtesy Selmer Halvorsen, p. 73). Front Cover, Inset (lower): Musicians in farmyard (Ronald Ahrens collection, State Historical Society of Wisconsin, p. 31). Back Cover: Everett Knudtson fiddling (photo by Lewis Koch, p. 106).

Quoted Passages

Passages quoted from the work of others carry numerical footnotes; further information on citations is given in Appendix: Notes.

Quotes which are not footnoted are from the author's original fieldwork. The individuals quoted are listed in Appendix: Interview Sources, with brief biographical notes.

Roll up the rug!

Table of Contents

Introduction   8

The Ways of the Fiddler   14

Roll Up the Rug & Carry Out the Cookstove!   42

Puzzlin' It Out   64

A Time of Change   82

Conclusion: The Kingdom of Fiddlers   107

APPENDICES
Notes Cited in the Text   113
Interview Sources   118
Photographic Credits   123
Further Resources   127

Fiddle and hammered-dulcimer duet by Otto and Ragna Holten.

Introduction

Always, smiles quickly appeared and faces shone with the delight of recalling dances and musical escapades....

Having worked sporadically to collect stories from elder fiddlers for twenty years now—and having talked for the last ten about finishing a book on this material "soon"—I hope it will come as a pleasant surprise to those who finally see this in print.

The words and photographs in *Farmhouse Fiddlers* describe an era of homemade music-making for country dances. This tradition of recreational fiddling and dancing seems to have been a fairly common pastime in many Midwestern farm neighborhoods throughout the early 1900s, when most of the folks I interviewed were young.

The stories in this book are drawn mostly from a series of interviews with musicians that I held in the years 1976 to 1985, which in turn led to growing friendships and many return visits since then. My first interviews started in the mid-1970s when I was trying to learn to play fiddle myself. Wanting to learn more about the musical heritage of the region, I soon found there was not much available, either as recordings or in print. If I wanted to find out more, it looked like I would have to go seek out some fiddlers on my own.

Nearly all of my fieldwork interviews were held in Wisconsin. Most of the musicians grew up in that state, and place names in this book are in Wisconsin unless otherwise noted in the text. However, some of the fiddlers I talked with had lived in nearby states, and material I collected seems to match well with that documented by others elsewhere across the region. I hope this book can give a general overview of homemade rural music in the Midwest, while recognizing there are many local variants depending on settlement patterns, types of farming, and ethnic and family traditions.

About two-thirds of my interviews came from a band of counties stretching from south-central Wisconsin in an arc through west-central Wisconsin. This region of family farms was an especially rich area musically. Many of the small farms are nestled in beautiful hill country, an unglaciated land interlaced with steep creek valleys, known locally as "hollows" or "coulees," divided by scenic ridges and hilltops with grand vistas. Centers of in-depth study included the towns of Stoughton, Westby and Viroqua, and Blair.

Wherever I traveled, finding a lot of elder fiddlers turned

out to be much easier than I expected. All I had to do was stop in small towns—at general stores, gas stations, taverns, or cafes—and ask about local fiddlers "who used to play back in the 'house party' days." Mentioning the phrase "house party" to an old-timer invariably produced sparkling eyes, often a slew of personal memories, and the names of a few retired fiddlers living nearby.

When I tracked the fiddlers down, calling first or just dropping by and knocking on their doors, I discovered a few of them were still somewhat active, playing for occasional events like ice-cream socials, wedding anniversaries, or retirement-home doings. Others were retired, but had fiddles tucked away in closets or under beds, and still enjoyed occasional musical gatherings with friends. Some were no longer able to play at all, but had wonderfully clear memories. Always, smiles quickly appeared and faces shone with the delight of recalling dances and musical escapades from their youthful days.

Some interviews and music sessions I recorded; otherwise, I listened and jotted notes. I asked about old photos and gleaned photo-album stories. Besides fiddlers and other old-time musicians, I talked with dancers, descendants of well-known fiddlers, and ordinary farmfolk who had enjoyed the fiddlers' music. Some of the people now lived in small towns, but had grown up on farms. I focused on the rural memories, because it seemed from the stories told to me that homemade fiddling had played a special role for the farm families of the early 20th century, due to their isolation and need to form neighborly associations.

The musicians and other providers of information ranged in age from relative youngsters in their 50s and 60s up through seniors in their 70s and 80s. Some of the best sessions were with fiddlers and musicians who were well into their 90s at the time of the interviews. I recall especially several interviews in a nursing home with fiddler and accordionist John Hermundstad, who at the age of 97 taught me some great tunes. I have never been able to play them as smoothly as he did, gnarled fingers and all.

I discovered that once I found one fiddler, I had found plenty more. Each fiddler I met could rattle off the names of others, sometimes by the dozens, who used to play in the area. One early contact, fiddler Wendell "Windy" Whitford (of the Goose Island Ramblers band) invited me over to visit. When I arrived at his home he had prepared a list of several dozen old-timers that he had played with at one point or another. We started to go over the list, one by one, unleashing a flood of recollections about each. Suddenly he said, "Gee, let's just hop in my car and see if any of them are still alive and kicking." We did, and some of them were. Though I did not know it at the time, this book was underway.

Another senior fiddler, Selmer Halvorsen, kept a similar list tucked away in his piano bench. Drawing on his personal experience, the sheets of paper listed all the fiddlers who had lived and fiddled in a five- or ten-mile radius of his farm home in Lakes Coulee, near Blair in west-central Wisconsin. The handwritten list named eighty-six fiddlers. That included his own name, proudly written at the top of his list.

It became clear that back in the early 1900s virtually every farm neighborhood in the Midwest had at least one fiddler—and many had half-a-dozen who could handle the instrument. Multiply this by the thousands of farming neighborhoods in the region, and I found myself faced with no short-

Accordionist Ed Stendalen at home.

age of leads for a young—well, I was young when I started twenty years ago—would-be fiddler with a tape recorder and a willingness to travel a lot of back-country roads.

While trying to track down this ever-expanding batch of promising leads, a number of side projects were undertaken, including in 1979 the creation of a small photographic exhibit, with the help of a grant from the state humanities commission. To put this together, I teamed up with Lewis Koch, documentary photographer, good friend, and autoharp player, in what became a longterm partnership of joint research, fieldwork, and late-night homebound car rides from points across the state.

Lewis and I produced the small exhibit—and the next year, a more ambitious slide-tape program called "A Kingdom of Fiddlers." We toured this program around Wisconsin to a variety of sites, including many senior centers. The heartfelt response to the program was overwhelming to us. At each showing, people in the audience stood up at the end of the program to share their own stories and confirm the importance of rural house-parties to their neighborhoods.

In response to interest in the music, we then produced an LP record of old-time music, *Across the Fields*, followed soon by another recording called *Tunes from the Amerika Trunk* (see Appendix: Further Resources). By that time, I was working on a variety of other folklore projects with public and non-profit agencies, while Lewis's photographic career grew as his fine-art prints were exhibited in museums and galleries across the United States and in Europe.

Meanwhile, the accumulation of fiddler tapes and scrawled notes swelled over the years to fill several file drawers at home. When I thought about it, there was always one more person to visit, one more recording to make, one more reference to check. I am very pleased—and a little relieved—to finally find the time to complete this collection of stories about rural fiddling.

This is just one small piece of a large puzzle. The states of the Midwestern farmbelt are very rich in diverse folkways. In fiddle music alone, much additional work is needed to profile important characters and continue to document the myriad repertoires of old-time melodies performed by the region's tradition-bearers.

I would like especially to acknowledge others who have worked steadily towards this goal, including Bob Andresen, Tom Barden, Phil Bohlman, Andrea Een, LeRoy Larson, Jim Leary, Doug Miller, Phil Nusbaum, Howard Sacks, Charlie Walden, Stephen Williams, and others. Some products of their fine efforts are credited in the appendices.

Quotes drawn from the work of others are numbered, with full citations given in the first appendix. Quotes not numbered are drawn from my own fieldwork and are from interviews listed in a second appendix. I take full responsibility for the notation of all quotes from my fieldwork, including many passages not recorded on tape but written down by me, as best I could, during and after interviews.

I would like to mention in advance one aspect of the fiddling tradition that surfaces in the text. Almost all the rural fiddlers of the early 1900s were men, and although I tried to minimize it, I found it unavoidable to refer occasionally to the typical fiddler of the era as "he" or "him." A few fiddlers were women, but this was rare; the reasons are discussed in Chapter Three. This is one aspect where the tradition has been improved upon in recent years, and I am pleased that the present holds more equal opportunity for women fiddlers.

To Lewis Koch, photographic consultant to this long-term effort, I would especially like to express my great appreciation for sharing in this book a selection of his photographs created during the many field trips we took together from 1979 through 1981, and for allowing access to his documentary collection of historic images. The hours I spent at his kitchen table discussing visual communication and the philosophy of life—seen through photographs of old-time musicians, of course—were as enjoyable as the good times and laughter of road trips.

Also, many of the older images came from the State Historical Society of Wisconsin, whose photographic collections are truly outstanding. Special thanks to the dedicated staff of the Visual and Sound Archives, and to oral historian Dale Trelevan for helping me get started many years ago.

In particular, appreciation is due to the individuals who assisted by loaning images from private family collections, wonderful photos that show the many faces of old-time music and rural life, often in relaxed moments of everyday life around the home.

I would like to thank those who provided funding for research and interpretive activities which led to this book, including the National Endowment for the Humanities (Youthgrant Program), Wisconsin Humanities Committee, Wisconsin Arts Board, National Endowment for the Arts, and Dane County Cultural Affairs Commission. Thanks also to the many friends who offered advice, read versions of manuscripts over the years, and put up with my claims to be nearly finished.

Arnold Olson (1912-1982) recalls a favorite story.

Finally, I would like to dedicate this book respectfully to the fiddlers, who offered their music, memories, and hospitality. I hope these writings and photographs return a small portion of that precious gift of fellowship. I especially treasure the times spent with those who have passed away since we shared those moments.

Traditional culture is a field in which individuals may disappear from the scene, but their voices can continue... as long as others celebrate their memories by retelling favorite stories and playing tunes passed down, over generations, from person to person.

I hope the stories shared in this book will help keep that wonderful circle of tradition rolling forward.

13

14

Old-timer with homemade violin.

At this dance I heard, for the first time, the local professional fiddler, old Daddy Fairbanks... he was not only butcher and horse doctor but a renowned musician as well. Tall, gaunt and sandy, with enormous nose and sparse projecting teeth, he was to me the most enthralling figure.... At times he sang his calls, in high nasal chant.... I suspect his fiddling was not even "middlin'," but he beat time fairly well and kept the dancers near to rhythm.... He always ate two suppers, one at the beginning of the party and another at the end.

—from *A Son of the Middle Border,*
by Hamlin Garland [1]

The Ways of the Fiddler

God bless the man who first hit upon the very original notion of sawing the inside of a cat with the tail of a horse.[2]

PIONEER FIDDLERS

Describing his own 1860s childhood on a Wisconsin farm in the 1917 novel *A Son of the Middle Border*, Hamlin Garland summed up his disappointment in a town-dwelling uncle: "he could neither kill a bear, nor play the fiddle, nor shoot a gun."[3] Besides a substantial repertory of dance tunes and rhythms, rural pioneer fiddlers of the Midwest also inherited a rich, romantic folk image. In literature of the era, the fiddler is seen as a heroic figure with an exalted, if sometimes eccentric, spirit. His mesmerizing ability seemed to cast quite a spell on impressionable young country lads. Later in his novel, Hamlin described his favorite uncle, David, who did play the fiddle:

> This was the best part of David to me. He could make any room mystical with the magic of his bow. True, his pieces were mainly venerable dance tunes, cotillions, hornpipes—melodies which had passed from fiddler to fiddler... but with a gift of putting into even the simplest song an emotion which subdued us and silenced us, he played on, absorbed and intent. From these familiar pieces he passed on to others for which he had no names, melodies strangely sweet and sad, full of longing cries, voicing something which I simply felt but could not understand.
>
> ... as he bent above his instrument his black eyes glowing, his fine head drooping low, my heart bowed down in worship of his skill. He was my hero, the handsomest, most romantic figure in all my world.[4]

In the beloved children's books by Laura Ingalls Wilder set in the 1870s that make up the "Little House" series, Laura's father, Charles Ingalls, is the quintessential settler. He builds the family cabin and plows the fields. He shoots wild game and chases away bears. And in the evenings, whether in a little cabin in Wisconsin or sod dugout in Minnesota or small house on the South Dakota prairie, he entertains his family with stories, songs, and his fiddle-playing.

> Pa had tuned his fiddle and now he set it against his shoulder. Overhead the wind went wailing in the cold dark. But in the dugout [sod house] everything was snug and cozy.
>
> Bits of firelight came through the seams of the

stove and twinkled on Ma's steel knitting needles and tried to catch Pa's elbow. In the shadows the bow was dancing, on the floor Pa's foot was tapping, and the merry music hid the lonely crying of the wind.[5]

Like the flintlock rifle hanging on the wall or the Bible resting on a table, the fiddle was a symbol of the simple comforts of a pioneer home. Like the patterns of a patchwork quilt or the hum of a spinning wheel, the music of the fiddle was a talisman that helped to shut out the vast, untamed wilderness that began outside the cabin door. The fiddler's tunes echoed the cozy familiarity of the family circle.

> All day the storm lasted. The windows were white and the wind never stopped howling and screaming. It was pleasant in the warm house. Laura and Mary did their lessons, then Pa played the fiddle while Ma rocked and knitted, and bean soup simmered on the stove.[6]

As pioneer settlements grew, the fiddler's music rang forth at more and more community events. The fiddler played a key role in gatherings of families to celebrate, socialize, and welcome newcomers. An early settler in central Illinois, Col. Daniel M. Parkinson, described in his memoirs the traditional welcome given to new arrivals.

> When a new-comer arrived in the country, the settlers, without distinction or ceremony, sent at once to pay him a visit, whom they usually found in a tent or camp. ...in a few days, all hands... turned out, and built the new-comer a house, cut and split his rails, hauled them out, put them up in fence around the land he wished to cultivate, and then his land was broken up

for him ready for the seed. ... And to conclude these friendly attentions... a most joyous and convivial occasion was enjoyed, when the younger portion of the company would trip the light, fantastic toe [ie., dance] over some rough puncheon floor. Thus would be formed the most warm and enduring friendships....[7]

The small size of the pioneer cabin and its simple provisions encouraged a spirit of companionship, tolerance, and sharing.

> I remember once we had a gathering at my home, when the whole settlement was present, and although we had only a room of 16 x 18 to dance in, with Jeff Shaver as musician, sitting in one corner on an empty sauerkraut barrel... you can hardy find a jollier set than there was that night in the humble cabin.[8]

> ... the contribution of a few ounces of tea by one, hulled corn, etc., by others... and notice circulated, would draw the entire neighborhood together as with a magnetic power. The music cost little or nothing, for a goodly portion of the primeval settlers were fiddlers....[9]

The crude floor required some caution in dancing. At one party held in a log building with a "puncheon" floor—hewn logs laid on supporting sills, with sizable gaps between the logs—a visiting Swede tried to explain that it was like "dancing over canals." [10]

At an early-settlers ball in southern Wisconsin, the dance held in an upstairs garret required care in arrangement so that "the taller persons were considerately accorded positions beneath the ridgepole." [11] Such gatherings offered a chance

Pioneer homestead, 1870s.

The good people of the county were my firm friends. The citizens of the town were all clever. I had no real enemies any where, so far as I knew. We had social dancing parties frequently, sometimes in the town at Francis Meeha's hotel at a dollar a couple, sometimes at farmers's houses in the country after a chopping match by the neighboring men and quilting party by the women, winding up with contre dances by the girls and boys in the evening. Everyone knew every other body, all were on their best behavior and all were happy.

Daniel Harmon Brush,
*Growing Up with Southern Illinois:
1820 to 1861* [12]

"...a goodly portion of the primeval settlers were fiddlers."

Wedding on a farm, late 1890s.

for young men to survey the opportunities to attract a spouse. At the above-mentioned garret dance, each of the three unmarried women in attendance "received an offer of marriage from a young farmer of the neighborhood. One of them accepted and the wedding followed within a fortnight." [13]

At the pioneer wedding, the happy union was given a seal of community approval by the dancing which followed. The sound of "rosin the bow" was the signal to begin, and the tromp of heavy boots and swirl of petticoats could be heard far into the night. The following account from 1838 tells of the first wedding held in Madison, Wisconsin, at an inn run by Mr. and Mrs. Peck.

> ... The room was decorated with the early flowers of spring, such as wild tulips and hyacinths, which were found in great abundance.... The wedding presents were not costly nor numerous, but they were unique and useful in a young family in a new country; prominent among which might be mentioned a milk-stool, an empty champagne basket with rockers attached, and a fish-hook and line, labelled "to supply the family with suckers."
>
> ... The ceremony over, the cry was "On with the dance!" and, inspired by the thrilling music of the violin in the hands of Luther Peck, a younger brother of the landlord, the dance went on, and "joy was unconfined," until the morrow's sun was well up to light home the retiring guests. [14]

As the pioneer settlements grew by influx, marriage, and birth, the bonds of community were joined and strengthened with each festivity. "Frolics" or "bees" to husk corn, make maple sugar, or pluck goose-down for pillows combined work and play. From central Ohio, an 1881 history described one such pioneer event.

> "Kicking frolics" were in vogue in those early times. ... The cabin floor was cleared for action and half a dozen chairs, or stools, placed in a circle in the center and connected by a cord to prevent recoil. On these the six young men seated themselves with boots and stockings off, and pants rolled up above the knee. ... The [coarsely-woven wool] cloth was placed in the center, wet with soap-suds and then the kicking commenced by measured steps driving the bundle of cloth round and round, the elderly lady with gourd in hand pouring on more soap-suds, and every now and then, with spectacles on nose and yard-stick in hand, measuring the goods until they were shrunk to the desired width, and then [the lads were called] to a dead halt.
>
> Then while the lads put on hose and boots the lasses, with sleeves rolled up above the elbow, rung out the cloth and put it out on the garden fence to dry. When this was done the cabin floor was again cleared and the supper spread, after which... they danced the happy hours of the night away until midnight, to the music of the violin and the commands of some amateur cotillion caller.... [15]

Besides frolics to shrink homespun cloth, the pioneers joined hands to help each other pull stumps, remove stones from fields, and clear roads. One Ohio farmer, a pious Quaker, discovered his neighbors "expected a dance and refreshments" for such undertakings and had to put aside his dislike of dancing and music to allow such amusements in order to recruit the needed workforce. [16]

A small tree was sometimes erected to mark the "topping" of the peak, a signal that the festivities were about to begin.

Traditionally, the building of a new barn was occasion for dancing and fiddling, as the neighborhood gathered to christen the fresh structure with a celebration.

It was called "fiddling up a barn." You could not build a barn without having a fiddler there to "fiddle it up." The fiddler would play while the men worked, and he would sing, and they would sing, and they would stop for breaks and for lunch. And my grandfather Thomas [Croal, 1856-1962] probably fiddled up more barns in Sauk County [Wisconsin] than anybody.

—George Croal, *fiddler's grandson*

Lumberjack camp.

SEASONAL WORK AND MUSIC

Many pioneer farmers in the northern states sought winter work in lumberjack camps. At the start of winter, they shouldered their "turkeys" (packsacks) and left their families to head north to seek jobs as loggers.

There were many small camps scattered throughout the vast northern pine and spruce forests. Such camps were often little more than a rough bunkhouse or two, a cook shack, a filer's shack, and a few other crude outbuildings.

The pay was poor and hours were long. The traditional cry of "Daylight in the swamp!" rousted the men before the sun came up. They ate their meal in near silence, enforced by cooks whose job was to feed the men, not encourage conversation. Then, the men picked up their saws and axes, sharpened overnight by the filer, and headed out into the woods.

In the evening, they ate quickly and often headed early to bed, to catch a little slumber before the next cry of "Daylight in the swamp!"

Though the work was rugged, Saturday nights were evenings for fun, as Sunday was a rest day. Sometimes the men held jig-dancing competitions, or, if they were close to a nearby town, a few wagonloads of visitors, perhaps with some closely-chaperoned women, might show up for a dance.

If no women were present, the men on occasion held stag dances, stepping out quadrilles in their spiked boots. The loggers taking the place of women in the set might don red handkerchiefs, wrapped around burly arms. The near-chaos of a lumberjack quadrille was said to be nearly indistinguishable from a brawl—which was another form of lumberjack amusement.

The crews were composed of men from many nationalities. It was fertile mixing ground, as new immigrants were exposed to each other's language, music, and habits.[17] Fellows returned home to their families in the spring with a little cash

21

Sharing tales and tunes.

leisure time singing, card playing and dancing, that was not all. There was also violin playing and dancing, as there were no less than four fiddlers in the crew. Real musicians though were lacking, but in logging camp we were not particular about the quality of music.

[In the spring]... We returned home and found our wives in good health although, now and then, they had found difficulty getting food and wood. ...you can be sure Nils had big eyes when his wife laid a bundle in his lap and said, "There's your New Year's present." It was a pretty little girl.[18]

Other seasonal work that engaged pioneer men and women included berry and fruit picking, hops picking, and grain harvesting. The threshing runs of the Great Plains attracted many young men, and some women joined the crews as wagon cooks. Fruit and hops-picking camps often had small dance halls and encouraged the workers to dance and make music in the evenings; this pleasure was mentioned in recruiting advertisements. From these gatherings, fiddlers often returned with a new batch of melodies.

in their pockets and a lot of new tunes, songs, and tales.

Nils and I were newcomers. In the fall we built log huts for ourselves and our wives, and in addition we built a small stable for a cow we purchased in common. We also cut and chopped wood for the winter. Then we left to work in the logging woods. We had no particular destination in mind, but went north....

There were many nationalities in camp, Yankees, Germans, Frenchmen, Irishmen and we three Norwegians. In the evenings we had a big time. The Germans and the French and Irish competed with one another singing their national songs.... The Yankees also sang a few songs.... But we three Norwegians were poor singers and we often sat there like three owls among a flock of crows.

...While the lumberjacks spent most of their

Uncle Nels, he was a full-fledged old-time fiddler. He could play anything he heared. He used to go out to the Dakotas for harvest, you know, "thrashing," and of course he picked up some new tunes out there. And the first thing he did when he come back—he took out his fiddle and went over 'em.

—*Knut Volden, fiddler*

Good food and music helped keep a logging crew in top spirits.

On so many occasions—from loggers' socials to settlers' balls, from wedding celebrations to barn raisings—the fiddler's music brought joy to all who joined hands to create a frontier community. In return, the fiddlers reaped a harvest of hearty thanks, and sometimes other benefits as well. An account from Missouri underscores the value of the fiddle to the practical-minded pioneer.

> Papa's violin was among our most treasured possessions. It was a battered relic but a sweet tone resided in it. His grandfather had brought it from Ireland to Pennsylvania and his father had fetched it to Augusta County [Missouri] before the War for Independence.
>
> It brought trade to Papa's mill and store and got him elected to offices that advanced his business. He called the violin "Her" and "My Old Toll-Getter" for the percentage of corn and small grain that he kept when it was brought to his mill for the grinding.
>
> We might also have called her, "An Old Husband-Getter," for my sisters and I met our husbands while they were guests at dances at our home.[19]

FARM NEIGHBORHOODS & WINTERTIME SOCIALS

By the early 1900s, pioneer settlements had developed into more established farming neighborhoods. Winter continued to be the favorite season for fiddle-playing on the farm. During long months of cold weather, the menfolk found respite from daily fieldwork. In free moments, they might while away some time practicing the violin.

Certainly not all farmer fiddlers of the Midwest were gift-

Fiddler on his porch roof.

ed musicians like Hamlin Garland's Uncle David. As one woman described her husband's playing, "It sounded like someone cutting cabbage and humming through a paper comb at the same time." These farmhouse fiddlers, the plainest of "kitchen sawyers," played mostly at home for their own amusement—or as some said, for their own "amazement."

Winter was always a good time to invite the neighbors over for a dance social. Held in farmhouse parlors or kitchens, these house parties were frequent from the end of harvest in October until spring-planting time. At the farmhome dances, one fiddler reported, "It seemed like every other person there could play the fiddle." Most boys were able to scratch out at least a few dance tunes on the violin, while girls grew up learning to chord on the piano, a fixture in many rural homes since the late 1800s.

Other instruments brought out for house-party dances in the early 1900s included button accordions, pump organs, guitars, banjos, zithers, hammered dulcimers, and harmonicas. Typically, though, the lead musician was a fiddler, and in many cases, often the only accompanist was a second fiddler who provided a rhythmic beat by playing chords on two strings.

From dusk until dawn, farmers and farmwives kicked up their heels and sashayed about the confines of a small kitchen or parlor with an exuberance that belied their daily life of hard work. At the center of this frivolity stood the fiddler— or sat on a sauerkraut-barrel throne. As the bow sped and fingers quivered, the music led dancers through patterns of weaving quadrilles or spinning "round dances."

Who were these fiddlers of the rural neighborhoods of the

Father and Mother provide music for a farmhouse social.

early 1900s? What were their pleasures and personalities? Why was it their special delight to stand in a corner of a trembling farmhouse floor, sawing out music—week after week, year after year—for the dancing of friends?

In some ways, the farmhouse fiddlers were as different from one to the next as their renditions of favorite tunes. But taken as a whole, the recollections shared by country fiddlers of the early 1900s paint a picture of a common setting: the rural neighborhoods of the American heartland.

THE MARK OF A FIDDLER

Grandpa used to play for all the dances around here—sometimes two or three times a week. For weddings, he would go as far as the prairie south of town. That would be nearly ten miles to walk there, and ten miles home. He'd leave in the afternoon and wouldn't be home 'til noon the next day.

—*Manda Mortenson, piano player*

One essential trait of a farmhouse fiddler was a willingness to play, and neighborhood approval was shown in frequent requests for services. The old fiddlers expressed pride, their eyes sparkling, as they recalled playing three, four, even five nights in a row. Rarely did a neighborhood fiddler turn down an opportunity to play, even if the only pay was a little friendly appreciation.

Me and my friend Bernard Everson, we were about seventeen. He lived about a half mile from me. And he could play the guitar and the fiddle, and so could I—so we could switch off [trade instruments back and forth]. That way we didn't get so tired.

They would call us up and ask us to play for house parties. And they would have somebody stop by and pick us up if we needed a ride, and drop us off at home afterwards.

Lots of times we didn't get home too early, either!

—*Windy Whitford, fiddler*

For some, this popularity could grow to be a nuisance. Playing all night for a neighborhood social meant long hours for little pay. Returning home at dawn only to change right into work clothes to do chores could wear thin. Many laid aside their instruments when they got married and began to raise a family.

My brother played banjo, and he was pretty good, too. But it got so he was complaining about playing too often. After we'd gone to bed... why, sometimes they'd call and want us to come and play for them.

And my brother—the way he was, when he was going to bed at nine o'clock, that was it—he was in bed. And he said, "I'm going to sell my banjo. I don't want to get up...!"

—*Selmer Torger, fiddler*

After I got married, I gave it up. Farming is too much work to be out late, and coming home in the morning and having to go out and do chores.

My wife would get out of bed to answer the phone, and she'd come back—"It's for you. They want you to get your fiddle and get over there!"

—*Elmer Gald, fiddler*

Another important facet of a skillful fiddler was the ability to "play all night long and never repeat a tune." Knowing only a few tunes was the sign of a rank beginner. Playing nearly non-stop from sunset until sunrise the next morning was the sign of a master musician, and required a repertory of hundreds of tunes.

It was my first big wedding, on a farm down in Beaver Crick. I was seventeen years old. They had a spring-fed pond there, and they had over 40 barrels of beer sunk in that spring. It was a big wedding.

When we started to play for the dance [in the barn], the sun was going down and shining through the cracks... right in our eyes.

Anton Tomten orchestra.

Andy served for four years in the Union Army during the Civil War, playing the fife. At home, he was considered the best fiddler in the area and was in great demand for dances, to which he often walked several miles, regardless of the weather. To make the time pass more quickly, he liked to play the fiddle as he walked.

[He made] an interesting device… so that he could fiddle even while walking in the rain: a waterproof, rigid hood made of shellacked and painted burlap which extended from his head out beyond his fiddle.

—Arnold Sharp, fiddler, telling of his grandfather, Andy Sharp, who emigrated from England to Ohio in the early 1800s. [20]

28

Musical memorabilia.

And when we finished, the sun was shining through the cracks... in the wall behind us.

And we never played the same tune twice.

—*Selmer Halvorsen, fiddler*

Besides knowing lots of tunes, it was essential to be able to keep a steady beat. A fiddler was expected to put a liveliness in the music, but not at the cost of losing the right "swing," or "the time" in the tune. Some musicians had that innate sense of tempo. Others, to the chagrin of dancers and fellow musicians, did not.

When I played [guitar] with my father [a fiddler]—we had in my home town a fellow named John McFarland. And he was the best waltzer I'd ever seen on the floor. And when he started to waltz, I picked up his time. So we kept that time.

Sometimes a fiddle player will gain time—speed up, you know. My father never did. When you started, you finished at the same pace.

—*Rudy Everson, guitar player*

A lot of old fellows that picked it up by ear, they get into such bad habits and they don't quite finish out the last measure. And they'll throw you out of step when you're waltzing, so bad, see. Or they'll hold it over extry long—it'll raise the divil, too!

They wanted me to "second" [back-up on piano] for this fellow, this Ward. Oh, he was just as ruthless as he could be on the violin. And anyway, he was playing a waltz and I was a-followin' him the best I could.

And after one of the rest beats I says, "Say, gentleman, you aren't a-finishin' out your last measure on those waltzes. You're puttin' your dancers all out of step."

"Oh, am I?" says he.

And so he got up and placed his foot on that piano seat bench right behind me. Now I was workin' away like a good fellow and the rosin off that fiddle bow was goin' right down the back of my neck.

He did a lot better when he watched the chords. Course, I was just a kid and he was a middle-aged man. Maybe I shouldn't have been chastisin' him.

—*Charlie Bannen, piano player* [21]

Occasionally, a spirit of friendly competition might rise between a fiddler and the best dancers. A brisk polka might prove a test of balance, especially in the confines of a small kitchen where walls went whizzing past a spinning couple at great speed. Even a waltz, if played long enough, could become a real showdown.

Selmer Halvorsen.

One of the girls on the farm where I worked was engaged to a fellow. And he set up a dance party one night. It was quite a few miles away—I think about eight miles. We started to dance about nine o'clock, and danced and danced. Nothing else to do but dance, see.

Well, this couple—he was a fairly good dancer, and the girl was "number one." So I had this slip of paper and marked down all those who were supposed to dance with her. Otherwise, I wouldn't remember, and then there would be sore feelings.

So this couple was dancing, along with a number of others, and I was playing the violin. And all of a sudden, one couple quit, and another quit, and the other one quit... and so on, until this couple was alone on the floor.

So I kept on playing. As long as there was dancing, I played, you see. All of a sudden, a couple came back again, and another one came back on the dance floor. Soon, it was full again. And I kept on playing. And they all danced.

And [after a while] this second bunch quit, and went off. And I was still playing. Then I got the idea, "Now, I'm going to see if I can play you two off the floor."

It was a waltz that was easy to play. And, all of a sudden, there comes another couple on, and another. This was the third time, see. And they [the original couple] were still dancing the same waltz.

I don't know how long I played, but I know I played over half an hour without a stop. And pretty soon, they were the only couple left. Three sets had come on and come off.

And then the mother comes and she took the bow out of my hand. "Now, Jan," she says, "You quit."

On their way to play for a wedding.

Well... she had the bow, and I had to quit. And then the music stopped, those two [dancers] separated, and—one of them [went] this way, and the other, that way—somebody had to help them, catch them so they didn't fall down.

As long as they hung together, they danced perfectly. But when I stopped, it was just like you had two fence posts and took them apart.

But they were still dancing when that old lady took the bow.

—*John Hermundstad, fiddler*

Neighborhood musicians in farmyard, late 1800s.

MUSIC, MAGIC, AND MISCHIEF

The colorful character of the fiddler in the Midwest and across America is in part a lingering effect of age-old legends brought to this country from Europe. In Old World folklore, music was often associated with magic. In many places across Europe, local legends told of magical instruments, mesmerizing tunes, nocturnal meetings with "little people" or devilish apparitions, and enchanted dances.[22]

Fiddler legends were brought to North America with early settlers and soldiers from the British Isles and France, whose descendants were joined in the Midwest in the 1800s by numerous immigrants from Scandinavia, the German provinces, and elsewhere in Europe. The lore often depicted the fiddler as a mischief-maker, a good-for-nothing drunkard or eccentric who played the Devil's own instrument.

One type of legend common across Europe claimed that great musicians learned to play from the Devil. Fiddlers were said to have sold their souls in exchange for extraordinary skills or a magical violin. In older versions, fiddlers learned to play from "little people" or other supernatural creatures living in waterfalls, rapids, or woods.[23] One fiddler, born 1905 and immigrated in 1924 to the Midwest, recalled hearing such a legend as a boy growing up in central Sweden.

> I had just started to learn to play the fiddle. And I went to see this old man, and he told me what I should do. He told me—if I really wanted to play the fiddle, I should go down to this old mill that was down in the woods... on Thursday night... and take my fiddle with me.
>
> And he said, "Go down there after it gets dark, and sit down right next to the big wheel," you know—
>
> "and then, right at midnight, take out your fiddle, and start to play it."
>
> "And then... the Devil is going to come and tap you on the shoulder. And he will teach you some of his tunes!"
>
> Well... I didn't know what to think of that... but I decided maybe I should try it, you know. So I went home and thought about it all week. And the next Thursday, I took my fiddle and started down that road that led to the old mill.
>
> The road followed a ridge for a while and then it went straight down into the woods. And I stood there for a while—at the edge of the woods—and thought about it. It was so dark in the woods it was ridiculous. I knew just where that old mill was. The water goes crashing down in a big ravine.
>
> I tried to imagine what it would be like sitting down there—with all that noise. I wouldn't be able to hear a thing! I figured... if somebody came up and tapped me on the shoulder... I'd die! I'd be so nervous, I would just die, right there. Of shock!
>
> So I turned around and went home. I decided I could find some other way to learn to play the fiddle!
>
> —*Edwin Johnson, fiddler*

In the Old World, fiddlers often held low-status occupations—poor crofters, itinerant craftsmen or peddlers. Disreputable characters associated with the fiddle included gypsies and mercenary soldiers. Yet the music of the fiddler was in great demand at high festivities like county fairs or weddings. At a big wedding, which in some communities lasted for a number of days, the fiddler was often a master of ceremonies.

This odd dichotomy, of popular demand yet marginal status, enveloped the character of the fiddler. Local musicians added to the growing body of legends. Tuning their fiddles in strange ways, musicians in Europe (and later America) played melodies credited to the Devil, the trolls, the fairies. Eccentric and competitive, fiddlers could be jealous of their special tunes. Some even practiced ways to prevent others from stealing their music. The same Swedish-born fiddler—who almost ventured down to the old mill—recalled a charm used to drive off rival musicians.[24]

That same old man [in Sweden] told me something else when I visited him. He told me how to keep other fiddlers from bothering you. Suppose there is a guy you don't care for much... who is always coming around and wanting to play with you.

"First thing," this old man said, "you go out... and catch a frog."

Then you find a little box, and punch some small holes in the box, and put the frog in it. Then you take the box and go out in the woods and bury it... in an anthill.

You leave it there a few days, and when you come back, and dig it up and open it... there is nothing left but the skeleton. The ants will have picked those bones clean.

So you take the bones and put them in your shirt pocket. Then, when this fellow comes around that you don't like—you let him take out his fiddle and start to tune it. And when he's doing that, you reach in your pocket, and take one of those bones, and break it in two.

And then... his strings will snap right off his fiddle!
—*Edwin Johnson, fiddler*

Edwin Johnson (on right) and partner as young fiddlers in Sweden, early 1920s.

With links to magic, superstition, and carousing, Old World fiddlers came under attack during waves of pietism which swept Europe. To the English Puritans of the 1500s, idle pursuits like fiddling and dancing were unseemly and frivolous. Similarly, to the Scandinavian pietists of the mid-1800s, all forms of merriment from playing cards to whistling

33

or laughing were considered dangerous distractions.[25]

The fiddler's traditional role stood in opposition to that strict creed. Fiddle music was associated with dancing which promoted close physical contact between young adults. Drinking also was a problem, especially where rival communities congregated—such as at a county fair—often with disastrous results. One older Norwegian-born musician recalled the reaction of the pious to these wild festivities.

> You danced. You got drunk. You got into a fight. You got killed. And the violin got the blame for all of that.
>
> —*John Hermundstad, fiddler*

At the height of puritanical revivals, the fiddle was denounced from pulpits as the instrument of the Devil. Fiddlers were threatened with eternal damnation if they did not renounce "sinful" ways. In some places, heirloom instruments were cast into fires, smashed into tiny fragments, or buried in the woods.

> In my village [in Sweden], if they wanted to say that something was really bad—you know, absolutely bad—they said it was almost as bad as playing the fiddle.
>
> I heard some of the older folks tell—if there was a house where a fiddler had died, and his fiddle was still hanging on the wall, they went in with a piece of string, and tied that around the neck of the fiddle... and carried it out of the house and threw it in a fire.
>
> They used the string because they were afraid...of the fiddle's power.
>
> —*Edwin Johnson, fiddler*

Members of pietistic movements immigrated to the American Midwest, where they continued to shun dance music and fiddling. In some congregations, there was a fine line drawn—singing dances or play parties were allowed, but not dancing to the fiddle. The exact definition of "dancing" was also open to interpretation. One 19th-century account from Ohio mentions:

> For such derelictions [dancing], people sometime got "fiddled out" of church, or "churched," unless, of course, they could prove that they had not crossed their feet while walking to and fro with the music.[26]

By the end of the 1800s, anti-fiddler sentiment subsided across both Europe and America, and the music of the fiddler was tolerated and enjoyed by many. As one woman wrote:

> ... there were, then as now, some church ministers, narrow men, who ranted against the playing of the violin and all social gatherings that included dancing. But such opposition is grounded in gross ignorance and envy and we believed most firmly that such persons deserved our pity.[27]

Fiddlers also had a reputation for being as quick with a bottle as with a bow. Certainly many other community members were prone to misuse of alcohol. Fiddlers, however, were central to festivities where drinking was present, and although often poorly paid, they were encouraged to eat and drink their fill. If some fiddlers drank a bit too much, on occasion or regularly, given such a public role their flaws were quickly noticed.

Painted devils dance on the side of a fiddle.

The young people got around the ban put on dancing by doing a sort of Virginial Reel on the farm lawn to the rhythm of clapping hands. The old folks sat around enjoying the frolicking young folks. Some of the men beat time with their feet as well as clapping hands.

It never occurred to them that there was little difference between dancing to violin music and swinging and curtsying to the cadence of clapping hands. Somehow they felt that the violin was "an instrument of the devil." [28]

There was one fiddler around here—nobody could hold a candle to him. But he was a happy-go-lucky sort. Fond of the bottle. At a house party... one minute he'd be going great guns, and the next thing they'd be looking for him out in the bushes somewhere—passed out.

—*Gene & Mabel Volden, house-party participants*

It was the 4th of July, in 1913 or '14, and they had a bowery—and you ought to have heard those old-timers [play]. They had a good violin player there, but pretty soon he got drunk and laid down to sleep. So they took him out behind the bowery and laid him down with two other fellows [in the same condition]. They used one for a "pillow," and rested the other two on him.

—*Selmer Torger, fiddler*

With this reputation, violins were not always welcome in church, nor fiddle music at church-sponsored socials. Many Midwestern musicians sat in church through sermons where preachers railed against the wantonness of Saturday night dances. As one fiddler recalled, "I had played for a dance the night before, you know. I just slipped down lower and lower in the pew as he went on and on."

Yet some preachers appreciated the traditional role of the fiddler in community celebration. There is a story from west-central Wisconsin of fiddler Anton Tomten meeting the minister, Halvor Halvorson, on the main street of town. Having just conducted a wedding ceremony, and seeing fiddler Tomten, the preacher said, "Well, I've done my part. Now, you've got left to do yours." [29]

At the wedding celebration held at the farm of the bride's parents, the minister was a welcome guest, enjoying the sumptuous supper served to neighbors and guests. But soon after, the preacher politely took his leave, knowing full well that as soon as his buggy left the driveway, the fiddles would be taken out and tuned up.

A PART-TIME PURSUIT

Legends and lore aside, the typical rural Midwestern fiddler of the early 1900s was not a tippling eccentric, but more likely just a plain, good-natured farmer who had picked up the instrument and taught himself to play. Few achieved a reputation as master fiddlers. Many never ventured farther than a few miles from home to play for a country dance. Some were shy fellows who had taken up the fiddle because they were too afraid to ask any girl to dance. Others said the opposite, "All I had to do was to go up and borrow the fiddle and play four or five numbers, then the girls flocked around me."

Mostly, the fiddler's role was that of rural craftsman. While few made much money at it, they used their skills to brighten up the home or entertain the neighbors. Often, music-making was just a pleasant way to end a long day on the farm.

After a hard day's work in the field, my mother and dad would play for about an hour before retiring for the day.

—*Ellen Wrolstad Mears, fiddler's daughter*

Whether it was considered an artistic pursuit—well, playing the fiddle might have been an art in the hands of some,

A toast to the health of the newlyweds.

Carpenter Gust Erdman and his wife furnished music for barn dances and house parties.

but not all. There was a wide range of talent among the country fiddlers, from the rasp of the kitchen sawyer to the smooth strokes of the parlor virtuoso. All might lay claim to the title of "Fiddler" with equal right.

As one woman said of the neighborhood fiddlers, "Maybe they didn't all come straight from Carnegie Hall. But they sounded that way to us—because that was the music we liked." Another one said, "It was mostly local talent. Well... I don't know about 'talent.' But it was 'local', all right!"

The pay was negligible. A hat passed at a house party late in the evening would produce a jingle of dimes and perhaps a few quarters. "We got paid a little, but we didn't do it for the money. It was for the friends you made, and the fellowship of it all," recalled one fiddler.

It would get to be, oh, two o'clock in the morning. And they'd say, "Well, we'll pay you fifty cents more if you'll play a while longer."

We'd get two dollars and a half, then!

—*Windy Whitford, fiddler*

Some fiddlers had a rural-based trade as a main source of income, which dovetailed well with their fiddling pursuits. Henry Everson (1874-1965) was a stonemason by profession, and a well-regarded fiddler. A short, stocky man, he was known as a hard worker.

My father had strong hands, all rough and calloused from breaking and lifting stones all day. And thick wrists from swinging that heavy sledgehammer.

I used to help him when he went to a farm to build a wall. It worked like this. When the farmer got up... we got up. And we'd work until he got through with the milking. And then we'd go and have breakfast.

And when the farmer went to his fields, we went out to the wall again. And then in the evening, we'd go and eat. When [the farmer] went out again to do chores, we went back on the barn wall. We'd work sixteen hours a day... and charge for ten.

My dad was a hard worker. That was his motto: work.

On weekends, we'd get called to a farmhouse to play for a dance. They generally started at nine o'clock, and we'd keep playing [with a break at midnight] until the farmer had to go out in the morning and do chores. Then we'd have breakfast and go home.

Maybe we got paid five dollars a night.

—*Rudy Everson, guitar player*

Carpenter Gust Erdman started building barns in 1900.

Besides supervising the work crew, he and his wife also provided music for the dance held amongst the freshly-raised timbers.

> There weren't many barns around here then. I built 'em, and me and my wife, we played for the dances at the raisings. Big crowd of about sixty men and women and children all came for the raising. At suppertime, they'd eat, and then went home and did the chores.
>
> Then they came back and had the dance. Me and my wife, we played for the dance. We didn't get paid extra for that, [but] I was glad I got the job to build the barn.
>
> I was all over. One year I had eleven men working for me. Put up eight barns and four houses.
>
> —*Gust Erdman, fiddler*

Fiddling could be an advantage in other occupations. Tavern owners frequently kept a fiddle or concertina handy behind the bar for their own use or that of patrons. Otto Rindlisbacher (1895-1975), proprietor of the Buckhorn Tavern in Rice Lake, Wisconsin, was one such congenial host and fiddler who always gave a warm welcome to visiting musicians. Lumberjack fiddlers headed north to winter quarters often stopped in at the Buckhorn to spend some time trading tunes with Otto.

Hans Fykerud (1862-1942), tavern owner in the southern Wisconsin town of Stoughton, also kept a fiddle hanging behind his bar and knew how to use it. When he took down his instrument to play, "It really packed 'em in!" Locals claimed that Fykerud would stand in the doorway of his saloon—perhaps upon the arrival of a train at the station located near his establishment—playing his fiddle to attract customers.

Itinerant farm laborers, sign painters, and traveling salesmen were known to carry fiddles or small accordions around with them on their circuits. This insured a friendly welcome in farming neighborhoods, and might add a few coins to their pocket—or at least a hot meal and warm bed.

Isaac Nelson (1891-1953) was one such fiddling peddler who sold Watkins products. With a valise of spices, liniments, and salves, he went door-to-door through the farm neighborhoods of his district in west-central Wisconsin. The rural families on his route knew him well and, upon invitation, Nelson took "no coaxing to play up a storm." He was known to bring his fiddle into a farmhome and leave his sample-case sitting neglected on the porch. Still, another admitted, "we generally bought something from him whether we needed it or not." Staying overnight with farm families, he gave fiddle lessons to their children and played for dances in homes,

Traveling salesman Isaac Nelson fiddles for a neighborhood dance.

Dr. Andreas Quisling (1859-1911).

schoolhouses, and town halls.

When the owner of a general store ran for the office of sheriff in Dane County, Wisconsin, in 1928, he was already well known as a master of the Norwegian *hardanger* violin.[30] The talented Harald Smedal (1876-1936), was always willing to play his fiddle for enthusiastic crowds of fellow Norwegian-American voters. Whether it was his stance on issues of the day or his fiddle-playing, he won his election handily.

The popular appeal of the fiddle had a therapeutic nature as well. A melancholy tune could invoke tears in the eyes of immigrants, wrenched from old-world villages where music was a part of family memories. On the other hand, a cheerful tune could brighten the spirits of the downcast. In this regard, the violin was put to good use in the medical practice of Norwegian-born Andreas Quisling of Madison, Wisconsin. Like Sheriff Smedal, Dr. Quisling had played the violin in boyhood days in Norway. Emigrating to the American Midwest, he studied medicine and opened an office in the early 1900s in Madison, where he established a loyal clientele among elder Scandinavian-Americans. He occasionally found a dose of his fiddle music to be helpful to his patients.

All the Scandinavians knew him, you see. They'd come from Minnesota, Iowa, from all over. My dad had quite a big practice.

Sometimes they wouldn't feel so good—and he had his violin hanging there in the office. They would say, "Can't you play something for me? I feel so depressed." He'd say, "Of course"... and play something.

And that would take their minds off their sickness. You know so many sicknesses are not true sicknesses—they are just partial depression.

So if you can make them feel pleasant—cheer them up a little bit—there's a psychiatric help.

So he always kept his violin in his office there.

—*Dr. Sverre Quisling, fiddler's son*

MASTERY OF THE INSTRUMENT

In the end, the sign of a master fiddler was the ability to enchant. As an acquaintance of fiddling sheriff Smedal said, "When he played a waltz—I don't care if you were on crutches—you'd throw them away and waltz."

The master fiddler was the one who could make a three-year-old child clap her hands in time to the music. When he struck up a tune, size-twelve farmer boots started to tap and wives grabbed their husbands and headed for the dance floor. He made the old-timers nod their heads and murmur, "reminds me of old Peterson."

As one fiddler pointed out:

40

It's not just the melody or words that make old-time music what it is. It's the memories that go with the music. A tune reminds you of friends you've known, and places you've been, and good times you've had.

It paints a picture in your heart.

—*Windy Whitford, fiddler*

"It paints a picture in your heart." For the accomplished fiddler, the skill was in weaving and re-weaving this tapestry of traditional music and memories. The audience could number in the hundreds of friends and neighbors at a big wedding, or in the dozens at a farmhouse dance party... or could be as small as one person.

She was bed-ridden her last three years. Then Kjell really made good use of his fiddle. He played it for her endlessly then. I'm sure, all the old songs they loved so well. He had time, then, to be home [he had been a traveling salesman].

We wondered how many memories went through their minds. She was 93 when she passed on. He passed on three years later, at 96.

—*Borghild Skaar, fiddler's granddaughter*

Being a fiddler was something ordinary, and something special. The fiddlers of the rural Midwest were simple craftsmen, and bearers of a rich, complex tradition. There was a little magic, perhaps, in every tune. But however plain or fancy the melodies, however great or small their skills, the fiddlers played with a great deal of pride.

From beardless youth to old veteran, from stonemason to farmhand to traveling peddler, the fiddle was best employed to give the simplest of gifts: companionship and friendship. For many fiddlers, the favorite audience would always be the smallest circle of family and neighbors.

A jaunty pose.

42

On their way to the neighbors.

Roll up the Rug & Carry Out the Cookstove!

Oh my, did we have fun….

"Kitchen sweats," we used to call 'em!

You could get maybe forty or fifty people in there [a farmhouse]—all the neighbors, and their kids, and maybe a visiting relative or two.

If there were too many people to dance all at once, they just took numbers. When they called your number, why, it was your turn then to get out on the floor.

Old Andy would be there in the corner, fiddlin' away and calling out figures for the dancers... and maybe tradin' horses out of the corner of his mouth.

Before we started to dance we always turned [the picture of] "The Last Supper" around to face the wall….

There was always a pot of coffee on the stove, and maybe someone had baked a pie.

Even in the winter the windows would all be wide open, with the curtains carried out by the breeze, 'cause it was so hot inside….

There would be about 25 or 30 people there. During the dancing, the children would sit on the steps of the open stairway and gaze through the "spokes." Sometimes it was hard for the younger ones to stay awake for the serving of the food. Some couldn't, and they would fall asleep atop coats piled on the beds upstairs.

Uncle Rasmus... would sometimes take one of us children out on the dance floor, give us a whirl around. Our feet never touched the floor once... well, maybe once or twice.

House parties. Oh my, did we have fun in those days!

—diverse sources [31]

The dance party held in farmhouse kitchen or parlor was perhaps the most frequent form of rural wintertime recreation from the early 1900s through the Great Depression. Called "house parties" or, picturesquely, "kitchen sweats," these country gatherings were an excuse for nearby families to get together to make music, dance, and just socialize.

As neighbors arrived by sleigh and on foot at a chosen farmhouse, fiddles and other instruments were taken out and tuned up. Those eager to dance helped move furniture onto a back porch or into the yard, while Mother carefully put family china and sentimental knick-knacks away in a safe spot. Others took care of food being brought in, putting most aside for a late-night "lunch," and started a pot of coffee. The rug was rolled up, and even the kitchen cookstove, or the round pot-bellied parlor stove, was disconnected from its chimney-pipe and carried out the door by a team of willing fellows.

When all was ready, couples took their places on the bare floor, ready for the first stroke of the fiddle. With the echoing kerplunk of a banjo and the first wheezy chord of the pump organ in the corner, the dance was underway. For many hours, long into the darkness of a winter evening, the floors and walls of the farmhouse would sway to the pulse of waltz, schottische, and polka, to the strains of quadrilles, squares, and old-fashioned set dances.

House parties... sure! Rolled up the rug and moved all the chairs out of the dining room. I remember one dance—boy, did that floor go up and down!

The next day, first thing... Dad went down in the basement and put in some more posts!

—Adolph Bach, house-party participant

THE RURAL NEIGHBORHOOD

The rural house parties were pleasurable events, full of frivolity and merriment. They also had a greater significance as activities that helped to solidify the bonds of fellowship among a given circle of farm families.

In the American Midwest, farm families were spread some distance from each other across the countryside. Depending on the landscape, each farmhome might be within sight of perhaps only one or two other farmsteads. During long winters, when the inclination was to hunker down at home to avoid the cold and deepening snows, the house parties drew together a group of nearby families to make music, laugh, dance, and share the warmth of mutual companionship. Such events helped build and nourish the rural community network so essential to Midwestern farm families.

At the core was the concept of the rural neighborhood. A neighborhood was an informal but closely-knit group of farm families who lived near each other. While these families shared many activities, usually the neighborhood had no formal organization, except perhaps a threshing association. Instead, the neighborhood was simply based on habits of socializing and cooperation built up over the years.

Varying from one neighborhood to the next, the average number of households was perhaps a dozen. Geographical features often played a key role. Separate neighborhoods were bordered by large woods, marshes, or rivers. In hilly country, a neighborhood might naturally form along a long, high ridge. Farms in a small valley would tend to group themselves into a neighborhood. In flatter terrain, farms sharing a road, or gathered around a key crossroads, would develop neighborly associations.

Over time, neighborhoods created focal points of their own, such as small country churches or one-room schoolhouses. The names of rural schools often reflected the neighborhood geography: Sunny Ridge, Round Lake, Brush Creek, or Pumpkin Hollow School.

Farm neighborhood seen from a nearby bluff.

Neighborhood picnic.

46

A work-bee pauses for
refreshments served in the field.

Other gathering places were rural cheese factories or creameries, where a dozen or more farmers from a few miles in each direction would meet daily to bring in fresh milk. As they waited to refill empty cans with whey for the return trip, neighbors would exchange weather and crop predictions, news, and anecdotes of recent happenings around the countryside.

Lines between adjoining neighborhoods often reflected settlement by different ethnic groups. One rural neighborhood might be predominantly Polish, with the next Irish, or German, or Welsh, or Bohemian. This was often the result of new immigrants looking first to settle near family and friends, creating small pockets of ethnic concentration.

Still, rural neighborhoods by the early 1900s were likely to contain at least some mix of ethnic groups, as early settlers sold their farms to move westward or resettle in other districts. Immigrant children grew up and married across ethnic lines. Norwegians might find themselves with Irish neighbors, Swedes with Bohemians, Germans with Yankees, Danes with Dutch.

The mingling was typical of the Midwest. With a need to be neighborly, the ethnic mixture encouraged the attitudes of sharing, helping, joking, and just being friendly for which the region is renown.

> Oh, yes, the Germans used to come to our [Norwegian families'] house parties. And we went to theirs. We didn't speak the same language, but we all enjoyed the music and the mingling. Their music was a little different from ours, but we enjoyed it just the same.
>
> —*Jacob Varnes, fiddler*

> In our playground games [at a rural schoolhouse], the Germans and the Poles were about equal in number, so they would form opposite teams. And then the Norwegians always sided with the Germans, and the French with the Poles.
>
> —*Ruth Zemke Flaker, house-party participant*

The greatest need among rural neighbors was for help with work. The seasonal demands of rural life tended to triumph over ethnic divisions, drawing diverse families together into their neighborhoods. There were many chores that required much handwork. For help, a farm family turned to the families on neighboring farms.

> There was an area about two miles square, right where the river turned east and then west again. There were twelve or thirteen families that lived in that big bend, and we were just like one big family. There was never any trouble between us.
>
> We helped each other all the time. We got together for bean-picking, wood-chopping, chicken-plucking, little things like that. And then there was the threshing crew, and silo-filling.
>
> —*Emil Oehlke, fiddler*

"Bees" were held often within a neighborhood. Jobs too big or too boring for a single family seemed to fly by with many extra hands to pitch in and pass the time. These were social occasions as well, often followed by music and a dance when the work was done. At corn-husking bees, if a fellow found a red ear he was allowed to kiss the girl of his choice—if he could catch her! Depending on the season of the year, there were bees for apple-butter making, bean-stringing,

47

48

Threshing and barn-raising
were major undertakings for
farm neighborhoods.

chicken-plucking, taffy-pulling, wood-chopping, maple-sugaring, and quilting or sewing.

Overall, the informal system was called "exchange work," or simply "neighboring." The word was used as a verb: "We neighbored a lot with the Thompsons." Exchange work included not only workbee socials but small jobs like tracking down a stray cow, mending a fence, or butchering hogs together.

There were also large-scale efforts that required the cooperation of the whole neighborhood. Building a country schoolhouse, a church, or a neighbor's haybarn was such an occasion. Dozens of neighbors would turn out for hours, or days, of unpaid labor, working to haul, cut, saw, drill, and assemble as if the rising structure were on their own land.

The late-summer run of the threshing crew was an activity that often defined the outlines of a neighborhood. The threshing rings were associations of neighborhood farm families formed to purchase and operate a steam engine and separator, or hire a custom operator. The ring determined what fees to charge per bushel of grain threshed to cover costs, and divided up any profits at the end of the "run."

When "thrashing" time came, the men within each circle of farms followed the big threshing rig from place to place, helping each neighbor haul shocks of grain in from the fields, feeding the bundles into the separator machine and hauling the bags of threshed kernels to storage. Likewise the neighborhood women helped each other to cook the prodigious meals needed to feed a hungry threshing crew. After long hours of work, the men descended like locusts on the farmhouse kitchen, and huge quantities of meat and potatoes, pies and doughnuts disappeared like magic. "To eat like thrashers"

was a well-known folk expression.

Another neighborly interaction was borrowing or lending the needed tool or other item. This exchange could be quite extensive, ranging from the borrowed cup of sugar to a crucial farm implement or team of horses. From an early farmer's journal from 1849, the following account suggests a pattern of continual back-and-forth sharing.

> Rolled logs with Mr. Cleve's oxen.... Lent Ray Wright my rifle.... Went to Mr. Cleve's ashery to borrow a basket to get ashes in.... James Morehouse came for his tools.... Went to Israel Mangers to get a team to plow, stopped and hoed corn for him 3/4 of the day.... Went to Mrs. Hazelton's and ground my hoes.... Went to Mrs. Hazelton's to see about getting her oxen to plow.... Went to Mr. Cleve's to dig grave for his son John aged 3 years.... William Hughes plowed all day for me with a horse team.... Went to meeting where they was trying to form a Baptist church.... Mr. Frink dragged in oats on my land.... Put Mrs. Hazelton's clock together and made it go, got some cabbage plants from her.... Richard sick of the scarlet fever, went to Israel Mangers and got some sage for him.... Borrowed Mr. Adlebush's scythe and iron wedge.... Borrowed Rufus Manger's cradle and cut my wheat.... Worked all day for Herman Hazelton at digging mill race.... Borrowed 3 sap buckets....[32]

Besides work, a rural neighborhood had other activities and pleasures ranging from summer picnics to the annual school Christmas program. Wintertime bobsledding, sleighrides, or skating parties on farm ponds were popular events. Especially in the warmer months, Sunday afternoon was always a favorite time for neighborly visits, families piling into wagons to visit each other, be entertained, and look forward to the chance to repay the favor.

In times of emergency or dire need, surrounding farmfolk could be counted on to pitch in and help a family through hard times. If a neighbor fell sick or was injured, men from nearby farms helped with fieldwork and daily chores. Women prepared food and took care of small children. When there was a death, neighbors helped console the family, attended the wake, carried the coffin to its resting place, and brought food to the funeral supper.

Over passing decades, each rural neighborhood created its own distinctive pattern of life. Children grew up, and elders passed away. Some families moved in, others left. But each farm kept its place in the neighborhood circle. As the fellow said, "We were just like one big family."

THROUGH THE WINTER

In the late fall, Midwestern farm families prepared for the onslaught of winter. The work exchange ring lay dormant until field work started again the next spring. The harvest was in the granary, the fields lay fallow, and animals settled in to quieter patterns. Early snows on northerly winds blew across stubbled fields.

In farmhomes across the countryside, farmers entered a long period of lightened chores. They fed the animals, tinkered with machinery, fixed up outbuildings, and chopped wood. Still they found themselves with extra time on their hands to sit around the kitchen, read the paper, and watch the days grow short and cold.

Farmwives strove to keep the household clean and functioning, more difficult now with the indoor presence of children accustomed to roaming freely outdoors. For days at a time, heavy snowstorms and bitter cold might confine a farm family to its home. Roads remained unplowed, sharp winds rattled windowpanes, and ordinary diversions like books and parlor games grew stale.

Into this setting of cold and early darkness came an event almost miraculous in rural memory: the neighborhood house party.

As often as once a week in the winter, each family member worked to get evening chores done early and changed into clean clothes. Horses were hitched to a sleigh. Seats were piled high with woolen blankets, and heated bricks placed down by the feet. In slipped the children, scrunching deep into the cozy coverings. Parents took their places and off they went, on unplowed roads or, if the crust was hard, skimming straight across the fields to a neighboring farmhouse.

Lanterns were lit in the barn. As the family trudged from the barn up to the front porch, the house resounded with a muffled thump of dancing and distant laughter. Suddenly music burst forth in full gaiety as the door was thrown open, revealing a welcoming throng of neighbors inside.

> I remember the time we broke off a corner of the kitchen stove, four of us lifting it out of the kitchen to make more room.
> It all went right outside...the tables, the chairs, the whatnot, everything. We'd even take out the Round Oak stove. We sure didn't need that for heat once the dancing started!

As winter days grew short and cold, neighborhood socials were anticipated with pleasure.

We used to tie the pump organ to the running board of the old Ford— to take it up to the Overberg farm when we played up there for house parties.

My father, Fay Allen, would play fiddle, and my brother Morris played banjo, and my mother or I chorded on the organ. I was just 12 when I learned to chord.

—Ethel Lerum, house-party musician

52

Bows poised for the first waltz.

Nobody had any money. Well, where could you find a night's entertainment any cheaper than for a loaf of bread, or a slab of bacon, or a kettle of beans, or whatever? The home that you went to did not furnish the food. Oh, they might, you know, furnish the butter or salt and pepper, something like that. But everybody brought something.

—Glen Westphal, dance caller [33]

The dancing was always in the biggest room... usually the kitchen, or the parlor. In our house it was the dining room. At the Thomas's, it was the master bedroom. There we used to lift some of the smaller pieces of furniture right out through the window 'cause it was closer than the door.

They had the fiddler sit up on a chair on top of a table, so you could hear him.

All the downstairs rooms were connected, so you could waltz out through the kitchen... and around through the bedrooms... and back to the front room where you started.

Grandpa played the melody on his fiddle, while my uncle played chords [on his fiddle] and called out the figures.

Once... it was so cold outside, we decided to leave the windows shut. And the kerosene lamps just got dimmer and dimmer—we were using up all the oxygen in there with the dancing!

So we'd throw open the doors... and the steam would just ooze out into the yard. We'd go outside and cool off for a while.

About midnight, we stopped and had "lunch"— sandwiches and coffee, and anything else that anyone had brought. Everybody brought something, it seemed.

Maybe you had a sip or two of that "alcohol punch." All you needed was one glass of that, and you were ready to dance all night!

While the women got the lunch ready, the guys all went out to the barn to start up their Model Ts... to be sure they'd start again in the morning. And maybe they had a little fruit-jar of something hidden under one of the seats, and they'd have a little nip before they came in again.

Then we'd go at it again. I remember lots of times we didn't quit dancing until the sun came up again in the morning!

Around three o'clock, why, then the fiddler played "Home, Sweet Home." That was the signal to quit—he was tired, you see. But we would just pass the hat and collect another bunch of change. So he had to keep playing.

We'd all sit down and have breakfast together. Then it was time for everyone to go home to do chores.

I was so tired I just tried to hang onto the reins and let the horse find the way. Lots of times I fell asleep, but the horse knew his way home....

We had to carry our instruments home, and that was a couple of miles—sometimes more—to walk. I remember once it was so cold, and one of my brothers was so tired, he just stopped and burrowed into a haystack and went to sleep.

When I finally got home, Dad was just coming down the stairs. "Well," he said, "It's time to get up!"

—diverse sources [34]

53

A WHOLESOME EVENT

Most rural neighborhoods in the Midwest, except for those composed of strict religious groups that shunned music and dance, had at least a few wintertime house parties. Many had a regular series, as often as once a week from October to April. Even that could be increased with special events like anniversaries, birthdays, and holiday festivities, especially during the weeks following Christmas.

> The house parties started in October. And we had them once a week until we could get into the fields again in the spring. We might have a few more in the summer before the barns were filled with hay. Then, that was it until fall.
>
> —*Leonard Myklebust, house-party participant*

The rural dance parties were pleasant affairs for the whole

Neighborhood youngsters.

family. As one woman said, "There were no babysitters in those days. You always took the kids with you." The young ones enjoyed the get-togethers as much as the adults. They played their own games, watched the musicians, and joined in the dancing. Even small children were pulled into a square dance or swung in time to the music in a corner by a parent or relative. As youngsters grew older, though, a temporary bashfulness set in.

> We had house parties all around here back in the '20s and '30s. There was one neighborhood up on the ridge, and another down here in the valley. Us kids would go and dance when we were just five, maybe six years old. The adults would dance with us, or maybe we'd just dance by ourselves on the outside of the circle.
>
> Then when we got older, we got more bashful. When we were fourteen or fifteen, then it seemed we wouldn't dance at all, just stand at the doors and windows and look in. Sometimes we went to dances in another neighborhood, but not too often. The boys'd be bashful... and the girls would giggle... and that was about the extent of it.
>
> —*Gene & Mabel Volden, house-party participants*

Luckily, shyness was usually overcome when young teenagers reached courting age. Not only was the dance floor a place for recreation and relaxation, it was also an arena for romance. Many farm couples recall a courtship revolving around country dances—including getting to and from the dance in a suitor's sleigh or buggy, pulled by a team of spirited horses.

THE MUSICIANS

Most every neighborhood had at least one fiddler, and some had more. In the earliest days, dance music was often provided by a team of two fiddlers, one playing the melody while the other played rhythmic chords as accompaniment. The guitar was also a popular back-up instrument, as was the four-string tenor banjo.

Perhaps the most standard back-up instrument for a house party was the piano which sat proudly in many a farmhouse parlor. Often played by women musicians, who were most familiar with the instrument, the piano's chords gave a bouncy counterbeat to the fiddler's melody. Another common back-up instrument was the pump organ. With treadle-powered bellows, the pump organ gave wonderfully sustained chords and deep bass notes, very different in flavor from the percussive plunk of the piano.

Many musicians could play more than one instrument, and often just used whatever was available at a given farmhouse. On the other hand, musicians might go to considerable effort to haul large instruments—like cellos or bass fiddles—across snowy roads and fields to a neighborhood dance.

By the early 1900s, factory-made accordions were easily available, and over the years became popular at the house parties, giving stiff competition to the violin's earlier role as the lead instrument. Very common was the little "push-pull" button accordion, with either one or two rows of melody buttons. Called the "house-party 'cordeen," this small squeeze-box delivered a peppy, syncopated melody and strong companion chords.

Eventually, the piano accordion came into popularity,

A button-accordion player could easily fill a house with lively dance music.

although this instrument had its strongest influence later on the dance-hall scene as house parties began to decline in frequency.

In a pinch, almost anything would do for music for a house party. A harmonica could be pulled from a shirt pocket, while someone kept time by tapping on the kitchen stove-pipe with a pair of knitting needles. At one house party, the button-accordion player present knew just one tune, "You Are My Sunshine." But that was enough to keep them dancing two-step and foxtrot all night long.[35]

Ethel Lerum and brother.

FAVORITE SITES

While most parties were held in farmhomes, there were other sites in a rural neighborhood suitable for a dance. In early summer, a dance might be held in an empty outbuilding such as a granary, a tobacco shed, or a haybarn. Also, rural cheese factories often had packing rooms big enough to host dances.

In the warm months, a big event like a wedding might prompt the construction of an outdoor dance platform, or "bowery." A bowery featured a wooden floor of planks, and some had a simple roof. Generally they were gaily decorated with greenery and hung with lanterns for dancing long into the night.

One of the best sites for dances was the one-room country schoolhouse. Most schoolhouses had good-sized floors and relatively few pieces of heavy furniture to move out of the way. Sited centrally in a neighborhood for the convenience of children, the rural schools made excellent meeting spots for all sorts of programs and socials.

I remember one night we had a dance in the schoolhouse—it was really cold outside, about 20 below. We danced and danced, and nobody really wanted to go home... but around midnight we decided to "call it quits" and the fiddler played "Good Night, Ladies," so that was it. We got all bundled up and went outside, the whole group of us.

And it had been snowing, and the moon was shining... and it was so cold. Off we went, down the driveway, plunging in deep snow up to our thighs.

Well... we didn't get very far before someone said, "Okay, who's got the key?"

That was all we needed. We turned right around and went back in and started dancing again. And kept going until the sun came up in the morning!

—*Leonard Myklebust, house-party participant*

A "bowery" dance.

DRINKING

According to popular recollection, drunkenness was not a problem at the neighborhood socials. Strong spirits were often present, to be sure. Many remember a potent concoction called "alcohol punch," a mix of grain alcohol, hot water, and a little sugar. All agreed it was best consumed in small doses. To boot, there was sometimes a keg of homemade beer resting in a cool spring or milk-house.

In general, drinking was in moderation and its effect dissipated by the energetic dancing which lasted for hours. The presence of children, elder family members, and many neighbors put a damper on rowdy behavior. If on rare occasion a couple of fellows actually got into a wrestling match over something, "the next time they met, they shook hands and forgot about it."

The neighborly nature of the house party prevailed, from the music and dancing to the breaks for food, drink, and conversation. This spirit of simplicity, wholesome values, and familiarity fueled house-party participants through a long night of merry-making.

> They didn't have to drink to have fun. They were having honest-to-goodness fun with their neighbors. Whereas today, a guy will say, "Gee, I must have had a heck of a good time last night, 'cause I had such a hangover this morning!" It wasn't that sort of fun. It was more something... of association, and friendship, and fellowship with one another. That was the basis of their fun.
>
> —*Windy Whitford, fiddler*

Homemade beverages were often available for tasting.

SHIVAREES & OTHER OCCASIONS

A neighborhood also engaged in other festivities and shenanigans that might include music and impromptu dancing. Shivarees (from the French *charivari*) were an old custom of teasing newly married couples with nocturnal noise-making. On an evening soon after a wedding, neighbors would gather at a selected spot to prepare themselves for their descent on the newlyweds.

Noise-making implements were assembled for the attack. These included pots and pans to bang with large spoons, shotguns to fire into the air, and even circular saws which were carried on crosspoles to be pounded with mallets. Also employed were "Jerusalem Fiddles," or "horse fiddles," where a large dry-goods box with the top removed was rosined on its rough edges, then a small piece of lumber, also well-rosined, was drawn back and forth over the open top. "The noise was hideous and like nothing else outside Bedlam." [36]

The neighbors surrounded the newlyweds' house under cover of darkness, then upon a signal began to yell, fire guns, and make as much noise as possible. This continued until the couple was roused and came out to invite the crowd in for cigars, a drink, ice cream, or other refreshments. This sometimes led to a dance party in the home, as musicians often accompanied the shivaree with real fiddles and other instruments.

Most couples paid their dues cheerfully; others tried to outfox the shivaree gang by hiding somewhere on the farm. Woe to the couple that tried to ignore the crowd, as this only spurred them to greater heights, perhaps to return night after night until the penalty was paid.

In some neighborhoods, the bride and groom might be spirited off for a musical ride around the countryside.

> "Shivaree," we called it. Take the team and wagon and go. And we'd get a whole gang—the whole neighborhood—on the wagon. And stop and get the bride and groom, if we could find them. Lots of time, the game was they'd try to hide from us—try to get away. But we'd slip up on them and catch them unawares, and take them on the wagon and go for a ride.... We took them with us... and drove around the neighborhood for a while, singing songs and just having a good time, a party, a shivaree. I'd have the fiddle along, playing along with the guy with his guitar, and we'd ride along on the wagon playing.
>
> —Ralph Flowers, fiddler [37]

Other customs of music-making and house parties occurred in the weeks after Christmas. This was a traditional time for neighborhood visiting to sample each other's special foods and Christmas beers or wine. In Norwegian-American

Fiddle and banjo was a popular combination.

communities, small groups of rural neighbors would dress up in costumes to disguise themselves, and travel from home to home, barging in and clowning around while the inhabitants tried to guess the identity of each masked visitor. The tradition was called *julebukking*. Women often dressed as men, and vice versa.

One woman was surprised when she pulled off the glove of a particularly flirtatious *julebukker*, and recognized her husband's hand! He had slipped away upstairs in the confusion when the visitors came, put on a disguise, and came back down to join the fun.[38] With fiddlers in tow, the julebukkers often stayed to dance once they had been identified.

I remember once, the lady of the house where we went julebukking went and locked the door—so we couldn't get out again! We had the fiddles along, so we stayed and danced and had a real good time.

—*Bert Benson, fiddler*

FRIENDSHIP & FELLOWSHIP

The "kitchen sweats" were social occasions that reflected their rural setting. Rooted in a Midwestern neighborliness, these get-togethers were born of a frontier necessity to get along with one's close neighbors. With the work-exchange rings and other neighborhood institutions of rural church and school, the fiddlers and house parties formed a strong bond of association to help meld, and hold, a farming community together.

From childhood to old age, country neighbors took part in these activities, possibly without thinking about why or wherefore. They tugged on either end of a crosscut saw, and sat shoulder to shoulder around a quilting frame. They worked side-by-side to pitch sheaves of grain into the dusty, choking windstorm of a threshing machine, and sampled each other's pies, coffee, and sandwiches.

Neighbors pulled in unison on ropes to raise a barn-frame into place. They sneezed accidentally at feather-plucking bees. They banged on pans at a shivaree, and met to cut and split wood for the schoolhouse. They walked behind the coffin at the funeral of a departed friend.

And it was the same familiar faces who gathered in the wintertime to dance away the darkness, in a silhouetted farmhouse on a hill, the driveway marked with converging tracks of horses and sleighs from surrounding farms.

More often than not, the sun came up to find them still dancing. The exhausted fiddler would play "Home, Sweet Home" and "Good Night, Ladies," and the dancers relented and let him put away his instrument.

The rug was rolled back into place and the cookstove replaced in the kitchen. Children were lifted from beds and carried, still sleeping, downstairs to be bundled into sleighs. Snorting horses stamped impatiently in the snow and blew clouds of steam into the crisp morning air.

And they were ready to drive off, each family to its separate farm... but not until:

"Where shall we meet next week?"

"You're all coming over to our place. It's our anniversary."

"Okay, the Johnsons' it is. See you there!"

And off they drove into the freshening dawn.

House-party band at sunrise.

HEADING HOME

When I was a teenager, I played in a family band. And one summer I was working for a local farmer. And there was one stretch where we played for dances three nights in a row.

The first night was up by Dane. I rode there on a bicycle, played and then rode back to the farm again. And got up the next morning, bright and early, and went to work. Well, I was pretty tired that day.

So that night I asked the farmer if I could borrow a horse. So I rode to the dance the second night on his horse. When it was over, I rode back to the farm and it was pretty late when I got there. So the next day I was even more tired.

So the third night, I asked to borrow a horse and buggy. And on the way home, I just fell asleep and let the horse take me home.

Well, the farmer woke me up early the next morning and wanted me to do some cultivating [corn]. So I hitched up a horse to the cultivator and off we went. Before I got to the end of the first row, I was asleep again. The horse just stopped at the fence line and stood there.

After a while I woke up and looked back at the row I had just "cultivated." Well, it was quite a mess...I had torn up half the corn. So I just tied the horse to a tree there and went back to sleep.

And when the farmer came out and found me there, I just told him he should have known better than to send me out to cultivate after I'd been out playing three nights in a row.

—*Werner Hilgers, house-party musician*

Farmer and fiddler Fay Allen, front center, with neighborhood silo-filling crew, 1920s.

62

Fiddler by lamplight, 1930s.

64

Young fiddler on an outing.

Puzzlin' It Out

Music self played is happiness self made.
—Sears, Roebuck catalog, 1927

CHILDHOOD MEMORIES

I get a kick out of telling people that my fiddle teacher was born in 1849. "1949?" they say. No, 1849. That was my Grandpa Smith. He had come to Wisconsin from the Berkshire Hills out east just before the time of the Civil War. He and my grandmother lived all by themselves down by Albion.

And when I was a little kid, there was a period when my mother was sick quite a bit of the time. And there were seven of us kids... so I got sent down to stay with my Grandpa Smith.

I thought it was kind of fun. Grandpa would always take me fishing in the afternoon. I can remember walking back for supper in the evening from the little stream where we'd go fishing. I'd be carrying a string of bluegills, and Grandpa would be singing one of his old songs. He knew a lot of songs that dated back to his childhood... all about people dying for love, and slavery and "darkies" and things like that. I was fascinated by those songs... by all those things I didn't know anything about.

We'd get home and have dinner. Then, later in the evening, after it got dark, sometimes I'd get kind of lonesome. Homesick, you know. And I'd say in a teary little kid's voice, "Grandpa, I want to go home." So that was when he'd get out his fiddle and play for me. To cheer me up.

He played the fiddle, and he played the fife, too. He knew all the old tunes... "Golden Slippers," "Bully of the Town," "The White Cockade," "The Campbells Are Coming," and lots of others that you don't hear anymore. He knew old tunes from Scotland—that was where his family originally came from, before they were in this country.

Then when I got a little older, I wasn't living with Grandpa and Grandma anymore. But I still went down to visit every chance I got... and I decided I wanted to learn to play the fiddle just like Grandpa. I must have been ten years old. So he started to teach me.

I remember the first tune he taught me was "Flow Gently, Sweet Afton." I don't know why he chose that particular tune—it's a difficult tune for a kid. But that's the one he wanted me to learn, so I did my best to figure it out.

A couple of years later, when I was twelve or thirteen, I entered my first fiddle contest, down in Stoughton. And I won a prize for being the youngest fiddler. Grandpa didn't go to the contest with me—he didn't go out much anymore. And when I came back and told him that I had won a prize... he didn't make a big fuss over it. But I could tell he was proud of me.

And I was proud of him, too. I thought just the world of him. All my brothers and sisters did too, of course... but it always seemed like there was something special just between him and me.

It's hard to explain. But to me it almost seemed like we had lived at the same time and experienced the same things in life, because we shared the same music and knew the same songs.

My grandpa was 76 years old when he died. I happened to be staying with him and Grandma at the time. I was thirteen, and it was March of 1926.

It's funny how you remember some things like they happened yesterday. He was teaching me one of his tunes that evening. "Buffalo Gals, Ain't Ya' Comin' Out Tonight?" And he put down his fiddle and said, "Well, that's enough for tonight, Windy Bill." That was his nickname for me—Windy Bill. And we went to bed. In the morning, he was dead. Passed away in his sleep.

That was a pretty sad day for me. The neighbors came over and—just like in the old ballads—they hung a black crepe over the door. And they embalmed him right in the house, and had the funeral there, too.

Later that same evening, we went over to the neighbor's house. His name was John Spence. He was a Civil War veteran, about my Grandpa's age. And he invited me and my grandma to spend the night at his place. And he had some friends over, including his son who played guitar... and that evening they sat around and made music.

And I just sat there and listened. It seemed like the first time I had ever heard guitar and fiddle together. It was just the most beautiful thing I had ever heard.

What with me being so sad and missing Grandpa so much, and hearing that music....

I don't think I could ever appreciate music like I did that night at John Spence's.

—*Windy Whitford, fiddler*

On the front lawn.

66

THE ART OF BECOMING

Childhood, says anthropologist Colin Turnbull, is the art of becoming.[39] In the rural neighborhoods of the Midwest in the early 1900s, many of the children were becoming both farmers and fiddlers. To a youngster on a farm, fiddling was more than an escape from the humdrum. It was a step up from routine chores and childish pursuits. It was a doorway to respect and admiration, an ascension to an adult-like state of grace.

Many years later, the old fiddlers remembered with pride the acquisition of their first fiddle. They recalled early attempts to "puzzle it out," and faithful attendance at local dances to pick up tunes. With remarkable consistency, these stories describe the rites of passage involved in becoming a fiddler in a Midwest rural neighborhood.

In the accounts, the foremost image is the mystique of the fiddle and its magnetic effect on youngsters. The stories describe Father's fiddle—left lying under the bed or dangling on the wall, just out of reach, forbidden to the touch.

We see the child standing just beyond the elbow of the fiddler, intently watching the motions involved in sawing away on the instrument while the dancers swirl in the background. Some of the kids who attended house parties spent their time dancing, or running around playing hide-and-seek. These youngsters did not. They were the ones who stood, and watched, and became fiddlers.

The accounts reveal the true teacher—not Father or a neighbor, but the sheer overwhelming desire to play. Anyone who knows children knows that once they set their minds on something which they sense is achievable, whether a cookie jar out of reach or learning to play fiddle, there is a very good chance they will reach that goal. Like water into sponges, the tunes and techniques of the old-timers were absorbed into the minds of eager beginning fiddlers.

An early start.

WATCHING & LISTENING

First thing in the morning, even before he went out to milk the cows, Dad would get his fiddle out and play. And when he came in for breakfast, same thing. And the same at noon. And then at supper time.

And the last thing us kids would hear in the evenings, as we were drifting off to sleep... was Dad playing his fiddle.

—*Bill Brager, fiddler*

Growing up in an era when music-making and dancing were common in the home, the average farm child was exposed to these activities at a very young age. Dad played his fiddle between chores in the wintertime. Hired men brought their instruments along with them for free-time amusement. Mother hummed ditties as she worked at the cookstove or washtub. Father whistled while he sharpened an axe on the grindstone or monkeyed with the clutch on a Model T. In the evenings, families sang together around the piano as kerosene lamps were lit in farmhouse parlors.

Melodies and rhythms were part of the natural surroundings of the farm child at home. Music was woven into the fabric of daily life. The tunes even extended into the world of dreams, as soothing lullabies floated upstairs from late-night house parties.

When it got late they'd send us kids upstairs to bed. But we never went right to sleep. Lots of times if they came upstairs to check on us, they would find us asleep on the floor... around the heat register.

We would lie there and listen to the music coming up from the room below, until we finally dropped off to sleep.

—*Helen Anderson, house-party participant*

The particular motions of the fiddlers, around whom the festivities seemed to center, soon came under scrutiny. The way the instrument was held, the manner in which the bow was grasped and music drawn forth, all this was the subject of sharp-eyed observation by interested youngsters. An old veteran fiddler playing away in the heat of the dance might sense a presence at his elbow and, glancing around, find a youthful shadow watching every move intently.

The rest of the kids—they'd put 'em to bed. But I'd be there, right by the fiddlers' side, right 'til the thing [the party] was over. Watchin' them. Listening.

—*Harv Cox, fiddler*

We'd sit on the porch t'home there. We had a pump organ and my sister, she'd play on that. And Dad had the fiddle. I'd just stand there... oh, I was maybe three or four years old. Just watching, and listening.

—*Gleeland Olson, fiddler*

"Watching and listening." Echoed again and again, the words describe the beginning stages of an apprenticeship. After this initial period of observation came the next step: imitation. For a child aged three or four, this might be with a short piece of a board held under a chin, and a stick with which to saw back and forth vigorously. Perhaps Father even strung a few pieces of wire on the board to simulate strings. But after a short time, this plaything was unsatisfying. It gave rise to the unavoidable temptation—the forbidden fruit laid to rest each night in its clasped case: Father's own fiddle.

I used to sneak Dad's fiddle out of the case when he was out in the fields. Mom knew about it, but she didn't say anything. She didn't want to get me in trouble.

68

Somehow, Dad always knew when I'd been in there. It wasn't packed back just the way he packed it back. "Uh-oh," he'd say, "somebody's been after my fiddle!" And he'd give me heck for it.

Until I started to learn [to play] something on it. Then it was all right.

—*Gleeland Olson, fiddler*

Considering the years of exposure to house-party music and dancing, an eight-year-old youngster picking up his father's fiddle was more than a true novice. Many tunes were already implanted firmly in the child's mind. From watching, the youngster had a good sense of how the instrument was handled. Combined with the desire to play, this could result in a case of spontaneous musical combustion.

We lived way out in the woods, in Dark Hollow, near Millville. My father, he used to play for all the dances around. At home, he kept his fiddle under his bed and he never let us kids touch it. But whenever he'd practice, I'd sit and watch him—like a hawk.

And one day, he asked me if I wanted to try it. He let me take it, and I put it under my chin, just the way I'd seen him do it.

To this day, I don't know how it happened... but I played a tune right off the bat. It wasn't perfect, but it seemed like my fingers knew right where to go.

Well, my father—he couldn't believe it! I couldn't hardly believe it myself. We both sat there with our mouths open!

—*Clyde Cook, fiddler*

I had been going to dances, and always sat and listened to the fiddler. So I learned pretty fast, 'cause I already knew all the tunes—I could hum them. Then all the kids were happy, 'cause we could have our own dances. I was eight years old.

—*Emil Oehlke, fiddler*

I told my daddy I could play the fiddle if he would just tune it up. He hadn't played for quite a few years. But that Saturday night he went to town and got stuff to fix it up with. And Sunday he tuned it up for me.

But I just put it away—I didn't fool with it at all.

Monday night when I came home from school, I started playing on it. I played 'til I could play four or five tunes... by the time my dad came home from work.

And that Saturday night, I played for a dance.

—*Millard Floyd, fiddler*

Watching Grandpa play.

GETTING AN INSTRUMENT

The next challenge was to acquire a suitable instrument. A beginner might borrow Dad's fiddle occasionally, but a real fiddler needed an instrument all his own. Luckily, a variety of potential sources lay close at hand. One was the "hand-me-down" fiddle, an old instrument retrieved from back shed or attic by Father or a sympathetic relative.

Such a fiddle might be a valued heirloom, but was more likely to be somewhat worse for wear. Some of these hand-me-downs had been dropped, thrown, or sat upon. Perhaps they had lain forgotten in storage a few years—or perhaps half a century. These relics had missing strings, wobbly necks, balding bows, and cracks in the body. Yet to the right youngster, they were prized possessions.

> ... so I wedged a domino in, under the neck, to keep it from wobbling when I played. But it still wasn't strong enough to hold more'n one string. So I learned to play that way—on just one string.
>
> When my dad saw how well I could play with just one string... he said, "If he can do that much with one string, think what he could do with four!"
>
> So I got a new fiddle.
>
> —*Milo Hoveland, fiddler*

In the rural tradition, to purchase a manufactured item, many farm families turned first to the mail-order catalogs. In the well-thumbed pages of Montgomery Ward or Sears, Roebuck, a variety of fiddle "outfits" were offered, crosslisted under both "violins" and "fiddles" in the index. The firms were quick deliverers and their goods were reasonably priced.

For example, in 1936 a young fiddler needed to send only $4.95 to Montgomery Ward to receive a violin (made in Czechoslovakia), plus "a good bow," a cardboard case, rosin, an extra set of strings, an instruction book, and a certificate for twelve mail-order lessons... "not dumped on the student all at once, as is commonly the practice" but mailed separately, one at a time, as the student progressed through the series. All for $4.95!

Thousands of such fiddles and paraphernalia were delivered to Midwestern farm homes. Packages were leaned up against the posts of rural mailboxes or delivered, often with a postman's knowing smile, directly into the hands of an eager youngster.

If $4.95 was beyond the means of the young fiddler, there were other ways to procure a decent instrument. One might barter goods or services with a neighbor who had a spare fiddle. One young fellow hauled a farmer's milk cans all summer to the cheese factory. Another chopped loads of firewood to earn his instrument. Others succeeded in trading items—from a "good pair of shoes" to an octagon-barreled rifle—for a useable fiddle.

In the 1920s, sales companies took advantage of the strong demand for fiddles among youngsters. Placing advertisements in family and farm magazines, companies offered fiddles as prizes for door-to-door sales of their merchandise. As a result, young merchants ranged through neighborhoods selling items like flower seeds, chewing gum, tie-tacks, and packages of bluing.

To their disappointment, the smaller-than-expected packages which arrived in the mail as premiums turned out to contain toy-like fiddles, cheaply made out of rough pine. Still, though pint-sized, the instruments could be played

From Sears, Roebuck and Co. mail-order catalog, 1902.

He was 13 when he got his first [fiddle], and that was out of the Sears Roebuck catalog. That old catalog was so opened up, it automatically opened to that page. So, finally... his folks gave him a fiddle.

—Agnes Olsen, fiddler's wife [40]

Free violins, advertised in farm magazines such as the *Wisconsin Agriculturist* (January 1925), caught the eye of many young would-be musicians.

upon. Quite a few farm fiddlers got their starts on the little "bluing fiddles."

If even this failed, there was still an alternative. Father would find his cigars dumped in a pile on his desk. Mother might notice a few wires cut and pulled from her screen door. A horse in its stall might turn a head to discover its tail being gently thinned. Soon, a young enthusiast was the proud owner of a cigar-box fiddle, with whittled bridge, pegs, and neck protruding from the realm of the Dutch Masters.

Outfitted with screen-wire strings and played with a horsehair bow, a cigar-box fiddle sounded pretty good—and smelled nice, too!

LEARNING TUNES

The next step was to build up a working repertory of tunes. Dance melodies were the fiddler's stock-in-trade, and they were fairly easy to acquire. A young fiddler simply went to a neighborhood dance and kept his ears open.

Perhaps he would be on the lookout for a particular melody, half-remembered from a previous evening. When that tune came up, it was a matter of listening carefully to the tune, to its peculiar twists and chord changes—and hoping that it stuck.

In this way, dance tunes were tucked away into young fiddlers' memories. Some had fanciful names, like "Ladies, Look Out for Your Shins," "Two Dollars in My Pocket," or "Tommy, Come Tickle Me." However, many dance melodies learned by ear came with no real title attached. If a fiddler was asked the title of a tune, he typically would name it after the musician he had learned it from—"Ole Johnson's Waltz." By this line of reasoning, Ole himself might know the same tune as "Selmer's Waltz."

If the name of a tune was not important, the melody was. With a sense that traditional tunes were being passed down over generations, many fiddlers considered it a sign of respect to keep a tune fairly close to the way they had originally heard it played. While each player put their own stamp of personality on a piece, many were also proud to acknowledge their teachers and stay within the bounds of a tradition.

> I teach my kids the tunes the way I learned them. I remember Mark [my oldest son] saying he didn't see why he had to be so fussy to get the tune just right—note for note. "Well," I said, "that's the way I learned them and that's the way you're going to learn them."
>
> Because otherwise—he changes a note here and a note there, and the next guy does the same thing—and pretty soon it isn't going to be the same tune at all.
>
> —LeRoy Blom, *fiddler*

However, melodies and memories were tricky partners. Unavoidably, tunes changed as they were passed on from one fiddler to the next over the years. Many musicians tried small "improvements" on tunes, and if their audiences approved, the new phrase became part of the evolving tradition.

Building a collection of favorite tunes was also a matter of personal taste. One fiddler might be attracted to a certain type of tune, another to a different type. For this reason, repertories of fiddlers could vary greatly, even within a small geographical area, depending on individual preferences of style.

Young musicians on porch.

Fiddlers became adept at learning tunes on the spot. Many claimed they needed to hear a tune only once to remember it—if it was a tune that caught their fancy. On the other hand, a tune which slipped easily into the mind at a dance could later fade away as quickly, stubbornly resisting all attempts to recall it. If you could only remember just the first few notes...

You'd be doing something completely different—days later, maybe months later—and suddenly you'd realize... you were humming that tune! The only thing to do is to drop everything and run and get the fiddle, 'cause if you don't... it'll be gone again.

—*George Gilbertsen, fiddler*

So I thought, "No, I'll wait 'til morning." I knew I should get up right then and go get the fiddle... but it was so warm in bed, you know. So I went back to sleep.

And in the morning, I couldn't remember how it went. I didn't have the slightest idea. That tune never came back to me.

—*Edwin Johnson, fiddler*

Ready and willing, fiddler Bernard Johnson at age 15.

Aspiring fiddlers might seek out an experienced musician to go over a difficult melody or explain a fine point of styling. Such a teacher might be a grandfather, or an elderly neighbor who lived down the road and did not mind a young fellow dropping in now and then—especially if he lent a hand with chores. Sometimes an apprenticeship might be arranged between an elder fiddler and youngster. Playing together for dances, the young fellow learned tricks of the trade while the master got a needed back-up from a second fiddle.

> Ole Johnson, he was about 50 or 60 years old and the best fiddler around. He sort of took me under his wing. I was only maybe twelve years old at the time. I don't know why he did that... except that you really needed two fiddlers to play for a barn dance—to make yourself heard.
>
> —*Art Samuelson, fiddler*

A more formal education in music could be sought from a local church organist, school teacher, or traveling instructor. However, although some fiddlers learned to read music and probably picked up a few tunes from written collections, for the most part house-party melodies existed outside of written music or formal studies. What did treble-clefs and quarter-notes have to do with the swing of an old-time waltz or the driving beat of a hoedown? Lessons could be disappointing and often as not were dropped after a few basic skills were learned... or the first paid installment expired.

Occasionally, Father himself took charge of instructing a youngster in the ways of fiddling. This had certain advantages. Parents, though, do not always make the most forgiving of teachers. They could be inflexible in their ways and were in the habit of enforcing parental opinions in an old-fashioned manner.

> There was one fiddler I used to play with—he was a short fellow and he had a funny way of playing, where he sort of stood on one leg and hopped back and forth from one leg to the other.
>
> I asked him why he did that, and he said he learned it from his father. Seems that his father played the fiddle, too. They would practice together, and his father would stand right next to him—and if he made a mistake, his father would haul off and give him a quick kick in the shins!
>
> So he learned to play... and was real light on his feet, too!
>
> —*George Gilbertsen, fiddler*

Sunday get-together.

76

Gleeland Olson (b. 1922).

I was about eleven or twelve—
I wanted to play guitar real bad.
So I sent to Montgomery Ward.
But for some reason, they sent me
a 'cordeen' [accordion] instead.
This thing come in a square box,
and, gee… I walked to the mail-
box every day, and I wanted that
guitar. And… it's a two-row
Hohner!

And before I got back to the
house, I could play it. 'Cause our
driveway was about a mile long,
see, from our house down to the
road where the mailbox was.

So on the way back, I would
walk a little bit, then I would stop
and play, and then walk. And I
could play a tune on that thing by
the time I got back to the house
with it.

—Gleeland Olson,
house-party musician

Conrad Larson (b. 1892).

There was a fiddler around here—Martin Erickson was his name. He'd be plowing in his field, and if a tune came into his head... he'd leave his horses standing there and go inside to get his fiddle.

My brother was the same way. We'd come in from the fields at lunch... and he'd have to go and get his fiddle and play whatever tune was going around in his head, before he could sit down and eat.

—Conrad Larson, fiddler

WOMEN FIDDLERS

Women fiddlers were rare in rural communities in the early 1900s. By and large, the fiddle was considered an instrument to be played by men. Girls generally grew up playing the piano, while their brothers "fooled around" with the violin. As one person described house parties in his neighborhood, "It seemed like all the boys could play the fiddle, and all the girls knew how to chord on the piano."

If asked why, some claimed that girls' fingers were too short to reach all the notes on the violin, or that they lacked the stamina to play lively hoedowns. This was hardly true. It is far more incredible that so many farm men with rough, large hands calloused from field work—sometimes missing a finger or two lost in a farm-machinery accident—ever managed to coax a smooth, sweet waltz out of a fiddle. The real reasons for the male dominance of fiddling had more to do with the folklore of the fiddle and stereotypes rooted in rural society.

The first problem was the lingering association of the instrument with drinking, carousing, and the Devil. Even if this image reflected more myth than reality, the aura made the fiddle unseemly for a woman to play. Men were allowed the latitude to adopt a devil-may-care attitude if they wished. Women could not. They were expected to uphold conventions of morality, which dictated they should play the piano—the instrument of church and parlor—rather than the fiddle of barn dance and saloon.

A second impediment to female fiddling was a traditional division of farmlife into roles according to gender. The men generally went out into the world to conduct business, engaged in politics, and took the lead in public settings. The privacy of home and family was the preserve of the woman. Socially, the men of farming communities were accustomed to playing dominant, outgoing roles, while the women played roles supportive but often less visible.

These separate roles were reflected in house-party music-making. The menfolk were more likely to step forward to play lead instruments, choose the melodies, and call dance figures. The women tended to play back-up music, while seeing to other aspects of the party from food preparation to tending the children.

These different roles are seen clearly in the many examples of husband-and-wife musical duos, a partnership common on the house-party scene. Two people were generally needed to furnish good dance music—one to play melody, the other to furnish chords to mark the beat. Almost invariably, this meant the husband played the fiddle, while his wife backed him up on piano, pump organ, accordion, or guitar.

There was yet a third reason for the dominance of men in fiddling. In rural communities, much music-making happened in the wintertime. This was the season of the agricultural year when farm men had spells of free time on their hands. In spare moments, they could tune up a fiddle and go over tunes heard the night before at a dance. With regular practice, they might become veritable virtuosos.

On the other hand, farm women had plenty of work year-round. Even if fieldwork was quiet in the winter, meals needed to be fixed, bread baked, dishes washed, clothes laundered and mended, rooms cleaned, children supervised. Before the conveniences of running water, electricity, and labor-saving household appliances, a woman's work was literally never done.

Women generally took tradional roles associated with the home.

Only a few women chose to become fiddlers.

One fall, Mathilda Saterlie worked in a cook car
[cooking for a threshing crew on the Dakota prairies].
A young man on the threshing crew heard Mathilda
playing her fiddle. They soon were fiddling together
and were married the next year. His name was Ola
Hove. Mathilda was my aunt.

—Rose Anderson, fiddler's niece

Randie Easterson Severson and her two brothers;
all three played fiddle.

There was certainly enough work to make a farmwife resist a rash urge to sit down and tune up the fiddle. At the end of a long day, she might enjoy playing favorite tunes on the piano as the family gathered in the parlor. As likely she would sit and sew while others made music.

There were no accounts told of women sitting around fiddling from morning to night, or being late to dinner because they were in the middle of a tune. As a result, at the weekly house parties, the women were less prepared to step forward with a full evening's repertory of dance melodies.

Although seen as supportive, the woman's role was not necessarily felt to be lesser. In fact, their musicianship was often recognized to be greater than that of the men. Chording on the piano—sometimes for different lead musicians—took more musical knowledge than playing tunes learned by rote memory. Most farmhouse fiddlers could not imagine playing alone, and recognized that without the solid rhythm of a good back-up musician, their scratching away on a fiddle was not really worth much as dance music.

Despite formidable handicaps, a few women did overcome the odds to become fiddlers. A fairly rare occurrence, a rural woman fiddler typically grew up in a family with a brother or two who played fiddle. Even when playing the fiddle, it often remained a second instrument; she tended more often to play the accordion or a back-up instrument. In public situations, if there were male fiddlers present, the woman fiddler might step aside and play only if coaxed.

> I played the slow numbers [on fiddle], but when it came time for the hoedowns, then I let my brother take over.
>
> —*Lucille Rowan, fiddler*

A musical birthday party.

No doubt the girls of a farming neighborhood could have learned to play the fiddle as easily as the boys did. But the social encouragement was not there. Still, the rare women fiddlers who persisted and passed that invisible boundary showed that being a fiddler was hardly a question of having the right size of fingers.

Becoming a fiddler was mostly a matter of deciding to be one. Most women did not. The uncommon women fiddlers of the early 1900s probably did not feel like pioneers, but they were.

82

Out for a drive.

A Time of Change

When asked why she owned an automobile, but did not even have a bathroom in her home, she replied, "You can't go to town in a bathtub." [41]

ONE EVENING AT THE DANCE HALL

There used to be a dance hall in Eau Claire, up on top of a little hill. It was run by a fellow named "Black Andrew." Black Andrew, he was nobody's fool. You didn't want to mess with him. But he was nice enough in his own way.

Well, this happened before I was married, before I had even met my wife. A friend named Isaac Williams and I... we went to Black Andrew's place on Saturday night.

And when we got up the hill and walked in, there were a couple of real nice-looking girls there. So I said to Isaac, "Let's get busy!"

So we asked them if they wanted to dance. Sure, they wanted to! Their boyfriends didn't know how, but those girls said they loved to dance. And off we went! I was a pretty good dancer, you see.

Well, it wasn't long before their boyfriends started getting annoyed with us. And they had a lot of friends there, and by golly, before you know it... we had ten or twelve of 'em after us.

So we went out the back way and took off down the hill. But we thought we'd try to do them some harm, anyhow. They had a Model T sitting out back

there, so we went out and tipped it over. Those touring cars, they were kind of light—there was nothing to them. And it went right over, and right down the hill.

By then we were in a kind of a hurry, so we had to go over the back fence. I was pretty spry—I got my foot up on top of the post and just jumped over.

Isaac, he was going to do the same thing. But he had brand-new shoes on, and he didn't quite make it over, and he tore his whole trousers.

Then, when I landed, I see something shiny lying there. And I stopped and picked it up, and it was a brand-new pocket watch! With a chain on it and everything—a gold watch, you know. Well, I picked it up and put it in my pocket. And off we went.

Well, the next day... I didn't feel quite right about that. So I went down to the newspaper office and put a notice in the "Lost and Found" column.

I had a room at the Ole Dahl [Hotel] at that time, down on East 7th, and that evening there was a knock on the door, and I opened it up, and there was one of those guys from the dance! And boy, when he saw me—did he ever feel foolish. By golly, you should have seen the look on his face!

Young rakes at the dance.

TIN LIZZIES AND DANCE HALLS

There was always at least one guy selling moonshine out back.... You didn't dare go alone. If you did and you asked a local girl to dance—you might get clobbered.

—*Rudy Everson, guitar player*

This family of brothers, they'd come looking for a fight. And if they didn't find someone to fight with, they'd fight with themselves. I used to sit up on the rafters and watch the fights below. I remember sitting up there once and watching three fights going on at the same time.

—*Conrad Larson, fiddler*

"Okay," I said. "Come on in." And he came in, and I asked him what the watch looked like—and so on and so forth—and he gave me a good description. So I said, "Well, it's your watch, all right."

He said he had come up the back way that evening at the dance, and had climbed over the fence, and it must have fallen out of his pocket.

And that Ford we had tipped over, it was his partner's Ford.

Well, he wanted to give me ten dollars—it was an expensive watch. But I said, "You don't owe me a darn cent. I don't want your money."

And he said, "Well, that's good, because I can't afford it anyhow!" So I asked him to go down and have a cup of coffee with me... and you know, him and I, we got to be really good friends.

And he said, "You know, the next time you come back to that dance... I'll be on your side!"

—*Sam Walker, dance enthusiast*

House-party fiddling in the farm neighborhoods of the Midwest reached a peak sometime in the Great Depression of the 1930s and declined rapidly afterwards. Like other changes in rural life, the disappearance of the "kitchen sweat" was not due to any single factor. Rather, the decline of homemade fiddle music can be traced to a combination of events.

In particular, the 1910s saw the emergence of several technological innovations which wreaked havoc on rural traditions of neighborly music-making and dancing. By and large, farm families enthusiastically embraced the changes as improvements to their social and economic well-being. However, by the 1940s and 1950s the tightly-knit life of the rural neighborhoods was in decline.

The first great rumble of change came with the appearance in the early 1910s of the snorting, honking, back-firing Tin Lizzie. With a toot of the horn, the automobile came rolling into the world of the rural neighborhoods. Many

Headed for town.

elders remember the sight of the first automobile in their community with such a vividness that they can date events from it.

Originally considered a pastime of the wealthier classes, the first "horseless carriages" were confined mostly to town life. The occasional cross-country journey was viewed with ridicule by a rural populace who still preferred to stick with horse-drawn buggies and wagons for reliable transportation.

This changed dramatically with the introduction of Henry Ford's Model T. The Model T was a mass-produced vehicle that was both cheap and mechanically sound. Introduced in 1908 at $825, by 1924 the price had been lowered to a mere $290, well within the reach of many farm families.[42]

With the purchase of a car, new horizons opened. For the first time, a family living miles out in the countryside could easily travel to town—to shop, attend church and community events, and enjoy new entertainment possibilities.

It was no longer necessary for amusement to hitch up the horses and jostle over to a neighbor's farmhouse, squeezing into a tiny parlor to hear an old fiddler saw out the same tunes again and again. The car was waiting in the barn to be cranked to a start and steered into town.

A growing variety of entertainers promoted their wares to a more mobile rural audience. Besides the occasional traveling circus and stage melodrama, there was now a veritable swarm of theatrical revues, minstrel shows, silent pictures, and an emerging attraction, the dance pavilion or hall featuring a professional band.

The halls and pavilions offered an activity dear to rural folks: music and dancing. But the halls were bigger, brighter, and better advertised than the house parties. Commercial dances became good money-makers, and establishments like hardware stores opened second-story dance halls. Taverns built on additions specially for dancing. Outdoor pavilions were constructed in town parks or at strategic sites in the countryside where they drew from a number of surrounding towns and farm neighborhoods. With motorized transportation, "going out" on a Friday or Saturday night became a favorite rural pastime.

We used to think nothing of driving fifteen, twenty miles in a Model T to go to dances in Fort Atkinson, Jefferson, Johnson Creek, Evansville, Edwards Park in McFarland, Maple Beach in Edgerton, sometimes to Cooksville. And some of the lodges in Madison had regular dances.

Over at Rockdale they had a place where they used to get some good black bands, with names like the Virginia Ravens or the Orioles. We danced waltz, foxtrot, two-step, and Charleston.

—*Orlando & Hazel Olson, dance enthusiasts*

Halls and pavilions did a booming business, drawing sizable crowds onto large wooden floors. Some enterprising farmers sought to get in on the action. They discovered that by keeping their haybarns empty during the summer they could make good money holding commercial "barn dances." These events were similar to the traditional barn-raising bees, only the new barn dances featured professional bands and paid admission. The following account illustrates the evolution of this new rural sideline.

I sold farm implements and barns—with pre-cut lumber and patterns and everything. And I knew everyone around the area. I would talk a guy into buying a barn, and I would help organize the neighbors to help put it up.

So this one fellow, we sold him a barn and helped him put it up. And we had a barn dance in it. For free, of course, for those who helped. Then he wanted to put hay in the barn. That was what he built it for. He had all his hay stacked and ready to go in.

But I talked him into waiting a week—'til next Friday—so we could have another barn dance, and this time charge and make some money. So we had a dance and charged, oh, maybe a dollar and a half per couple.

And we made enough money to buy a couple of tons of hay, if we wanted! So he left his hay stacked outside and ran a barn dance instead. And we were left out in the cold! He ran the show and kept the money. This was in 1924.

—Chick Watts, *dance promoter*

A PROFESSIONAL LOOK

Larger crowds congregating at centralized locations meant more money for good bands. It was a stimulus to go professional. This usually involved investing in stage costumes, sheet music of popular tunes, and promotional posters. The promise of good money was especially alluring to younger musicians with fresh, upcoming careers. Young bandleaders developed styles and chose names to reflect the popular imagery of the day, such as the "Montana Cowboys"—despite being neither cowboys nor from Montana.

Talented groups hit the touring circuit as road shows.

A commercial barn dance.

Traveling from dance hall to pavilion to barn dance, they crisscrossed the Midwest and sometimes ventured beyond. Other groups stayed closer to home, playing for county fairs, radio shows, and local dance jobs. These bands shared a common goal: to develop a professional style that would satisfy the new sophisticated tastes of town and country audiences.

As the size of halls and the crowds grew larger, the usefulness of the fiddle in these new bands diminished. The pavilions and dance halls were often big enough to accommodate hundreds of dancers. Even modest-sized halls, like a second-story floor over a general store, packed in rambunctious crowds.

In the noisy settings, the fiddle could not hold its own as a lead instrument. Before the days of electronic amplification, the thinner voice of the violin simply could not be heard over the din of the dance floor. The fiddle was still very popular in more intimate settings, as well as on the radio or for early

Thorstein Skarning's Orchestra, 1938.

commercial recordings. For dances, however, when fiddles managed to survive in professional bands, they were generally played by strong-armed fellows who had the stamina to saw away at fairly simple melodies and chords.

> I started off playing with a loose wrist, like my uncle. But when I started playing with an accordion player, then I had to use a stiff wrist on the bow, to bear down heavy on it, you see, to hold my own.
>
> —*Leonard Finseth, fiddler*

To handle the musical needs of the large dance floors, powerful instruments like accordions quickly moved to center stage, with ensembles featuring horns, saxophones, clarinets, and drums. Sweeping the country came the newest craze, jazz and swing bands, with their infectious rhythms and snappy arrangements. These big-name bands could pack dance floors across the Midwest to overflowing.

A NEW ATMOSPHERE

At public dances, the social atmosphere was altered as well. The hallmark of the farmhouse parties had been a cozy neighborliness. At a "kitchen sweat," everyone knew everybody else, and the whole family was welcome, from elderly grandparents to babies in blankets and baskets.

At the dance halls, things were different. The big hall or pavilion was cozy only in the sense of being crowded. The participants came not from a single neighborhood but from many locales, up to ten or fifteen miles away. Neighbors found themselves in crowds composed of many strangers.

Groups of couples tended to stick together throughout the evening, mixing less with other participants of different ages or from different neighborhoods.

> [There was a pavilion] up in Hixton—the Lakeshore—and one down in Independence, the Midway. And they danced quite a bit in the village hall in Blair, and Whitehall, and Independence.
>
> [The atmosphere] was a little different at the dance halls. I don't know just how to explain it. At a house party, it was mostly your close neighbors. But in a pavilion, you had more a "mixed crowd." But we had fun there, too.
>
> —*Arnold Olson, fiddler*

While young adults adapted fairly well to the dance halls, those much younger or older found it difficult. More and more, dances attracted a smaller segment of active dancers rather than a broad cross-section of the community. Those who came were those most enthusiastic about dancing and music, rather than just neighbors seeking to socialize.

To make matters worse, dance halls and pavilions often had a distinct undercurrent of tension. Rivals from nearby neighborhoods rubbed shoulders and competed for the attention of the opposite sex. Ethnic differences, less threatening within a neighborhood, were prone to insults, intended or not. With the added stimulant of someone "selling moonshine out back," dance halls often erupted in a flurry of wrestling or fisticuffs.

> We never went alone. Oh, no. I always had the family car, and we'd go four or five in a group. For protection. One was bodyguard for the other, and that's

The owner of a car had many friends.

planks put up around the hall on boxes for seats. There was none of them left in there when we got through, they went right out through the window, windows and all. We never even stopped to open the windows.... I was about 19 years old. I was old enough to know better.

We used to have free-for-alls, about every week in Bell Center there would be a free-for-all.

—*Frank Adkins, dance enthusiast* [43]

Some dance halls got a reputation as a place to drink and fight, and family attendance decreased. Even those who stayed close to home and continued to hold house parties discovered that rural neighborhoods were not as isolated as they had been.

Somehow, word would get out, and cars would show up from all over. People you didn't even know. And some of them brought booze with them, you know. It just wasn't the same anymore.

—*Agnes Rundhaug, house-party participant*

The close-to-home atmosphere of rural society had changed. Farm families found it increasingly easy to leave the neighborhood to take part in a commercial entertainment market. Though a boon for musicians interested in professional opportunities, the farmhouse dances suffered greatly. When asked to give a reason for the house party's demise, elder rural fiddlers gave straight-forward replies.

Really, I think it was the automobile that killed off the house parties.

—*Orville Rundhaug, fiddler*

90

how it worked. Some of the younger group, you see, came there just to fight. And most generally they were "obliged" [accommodated]. Most generally.

There was one dance hall upstairs in an old hardware store in Utica. You could go in there and dance all night for a dollar... if you behaved yourself.

I can remember distinctly... one guy came in there—he was a big fellow. And he said, "There's only two men in here—and I'm *both* of 'em!"

Well, he wasn't "both" very long. He was on the floor [in a fight]. And as soon as a fight would start... well, a good share of them would get into it. A free-for-all.

—*Rudy Everson, guitar player*

They used to call it Hell Center [Bell Center], and it was, too. I went there one night and it cost me $35.00 the next day. Well, we cleaned the house. I and four other fellows, we cleaned the house. Had a dance there. We got into a rumpus at the dance, they had

Bill Birkrem at home in kitchen.

91

We had fun back in them days, because we all knew each other, and we all stayed in a bunch—until them cars came along....

—Conrad Larson, fiddler

[Why did the house parties die out?]
[Without hesitation] The automobile.

—Selmer Severson, fiddler

first time! RADIO With NEW One Year Guaranteed "A" Battery

New Type "A" Battery....No Acids ....No Recharging...No Bother

$34.75

CASH LESS TUBES
$66.00 Complete
.....Or Buy on
Easy Payments
$5 DOWN
$5 A Month

Handsome Tarso Decorated Front Panel with Actual Reproductions of Costly Woods—New Low Drain Battery Tubes—TRIPLE Screen Grid Circuit—Push-Pull Amplification—High Efficiency Matched Stages—Rich, Lifelike Tone—New 1932 Model Speaker.

This new battery operated SILVERTONE is a real triumph of radio engineering. It is the first midget to be equipped with the new "Low Drain" 230, 231 and 232 battery tubes.

It is the first to have positive Tone Control. Better still, it is the first to be equipped with push-pull Amplification and the famous One Year "A" Battery.

Purchased elsewhere you'd pay up to $75.00 for a set of this quality! Yet WE offer it for only $56.00—saving you $19.00 at the very least.

New One-Year "A" Battery recuperates as fast as the radio drains it. All bother and expense of recharging storage batteries is ended. With ordinary care, averaging 3 hours of use daily, it should last more than 12 months. Size of battery, 13¼x6¾x9¾ in.

New Type Battery Tubes! These are really an amazing achievement. They give you performance that is every bit the equal of that of the finest A.C. sets. Battery drain is cut in HALF making "B" batteries last twice as long. Amplification is greater, and distortion is eliminated.

Exclusive Matched and Tuned Stages make ALL your tubes work at 100% efficiency—giving the performance of a set with many more tubes.

Six-tube TRIPLE SCREEN GRID Circuit, push-pull amplification, high grade 1932 model speaker, and tone control. Has sharp selectivity—and long range is assured by powerful screen grid circuit.

Cabinet is a masterpiece. Genuine walnut veneer with beautiful Tarso process front. Makes a striking reproduction in natural colors of rich inlaid marquetry. Size, 17 in. high; base, 14⅝x7⅝ in. Not Prepaid.

57FM1290C¼—Cash Price, less tubes and accessories. Shpg. wt., 27 lbs. **$34.75**
57FM1290T¼—Easy Payment Price ($5 Down; $5 a Month) **$38.25**
57FM1291C¼—Cash Price, complete with three new type 232 Screen Grid tubes; one new type 230 tube; two new type 231 tubes; one 57F5009 "One-Year" "A" Battery; one No. 57F5119 "C" Battery, three No. 57F5117 "B" Batteries and one No. 57F5517 aerial kit. Shpg. wt., 103 lbs **$56.00**
57FM1291T¼—Easy Payment Price ($7 Down; $6 a Month) **$61.50**
For Easy Payments, use Time Payment Order Blank in back of catalog.

Sears, Roebuck and Co. catalog, 1931.

THE FARMHOUSE RADIO

At the beginning of the 1920s, a second technological innovation appeared which, like the automobile, would drastically affect the patterns of rural social life: the radio. Unlike the car and dance-hall phenomenon which took families away from home, the radio brought new entertainment directly into the farm parlor and kitchen.

First appearing as battery-powered models, by the end of the 1920s a radio sat in nearly half of the farmhouses across the Midwest.[44] To rural folks, the radio was a marvelous device which brought an amazing variety of programs into the home at the flick of a switch.

The airwaves of the 1920s and 1930s were filled with a fascinating mix of opera, boxing matches, agricultural information, cooking classes, serialized drama, comedy programs... and the newest musical idols, the hillbilly balladeers and cowboy crooners. Broadcast from Chicago, the weekly WLS Barn Dance was an immensely popular show which spawned many offshoots throughout the region and had become a genuine national institution by 1928.[45] Featured performers on WLS included Gene Autry, Red Foley, Patsy Montana, Lulu Belle and Scotty, and many others, from Rube Tronson and his Texas Cowboys to the Hoosier Hot Shots "with their Jug Band Sound."

The cowboy craze caught on like a prairie fire. To the youngsters of the Midwest, the singing cowboys of the airwaves sprang right from the pages of the popular dimestore novels of the day. Every week, crooners like Gene Autry or "The Lonesome Cowboy" performed their ballads to enthralled hordes of young fellows, huddled eagerly around radios in Midwestern farmhouses.

The Hoedowners

Over the airwaves.

I remember, if I happened to be away from home when the Lonesome Cowboy's program came on, I would just stop at the nearest farmhouse and ask if I could please listen to him on their radio.

—*Windy Whitford, fiddler*

While hillbilly songsters like Bradley Kincaid and southern string bands had their appeal, they were outshone by the Wild West romanticism that gripped Midwestern youngsters. Evening after evening on the parlor radio, those songs stirred the blood of farmboys yearning for the fabled freedom of life in the saddle on the open prairie—or at least for a ten-gallon hat and a guitar. Young musicians absorbed the fresh songs eagerly.

A bunch of us young fellows used to get together in a park just outside of town. We'd sit around in our cars in the moonlight, and maybe someone had brought a guitar and would sing a song he just learned off the radio, and we'd all learn it.

—*Windy Whitford, fiddler*

In many ways, the old repertories of local neighborhoods and the new music of the airwaves were not so different. They shared many of the same instruments, chords, and rhythms. Only now, the "old-time music" came to rural communities from the outside, as a commodity produced and marketed for a mass audience. What had once been a home-parlor pastime became part of an entertainment industry. Some noticed a difference between the flavor of commercial music and the old-fashioned house parties.

I think the radio did make quite a change. It's just like... going to the store to buy a loaf of bread, or your mother or a neighbor baked a loaf of homemade bread. That was about the difference.

—*Windy Whitford, fiddler*

94

Kitchen social.

A SLOW TRANSITION

Over time, steady developments in agricultural machinery made it more feasible for a single family to manage a farm with less help from neighbors. Bit by bit, neighborhood traditions of work-exchange rings were dissolved. With the installation of telephone lines, electricity, and postal delivery across the countryside, rural areas became less isolated.

Through the 1940s and 1950s, rural one-room schools were consolidated into larger districts, and doors closed on neighborhood meeting places with names like Frogpond School. The years after World War II saw dramatic changes for rural neighborhoods. There was a surge in farm mechanization as farmers unable to purchase tractors during the war found lots of new equipment appearing on the market. Many young men did not come back from the war, and those who did had broader horizons before their eyes.

By the middle of the 20th century, an era of tightly-knit cooperation among neighboring farm families—begun a hundred years earlier in the pioneer communities of the mid-1800s—was slowly coming to an end.[46] Although some neighborhood activity continued, by the 1950s the independent farm had become the main unit of rural life.

For the farmhouse fiddlers, house parties were still popular through the 1930s (in some districts, as late as the early 1950s). For some years, kitchen sweats co-existed with dance halls and pavilions, with radio shows and talking pictures. For example, one fiddler recalled how he played on a Saturday afternoon radio show, then drove to a farmhome for a house party, full of neighbors who had listened avidly to his music on the radio before coming to the country dance.

The onset of the Great Depression, which struck farm communities in the late 1920s, caused a final surge of house parties across the Midwest. Low on cash, families retreated into older ways. They relied on homemade music, much like they relied on homegrown produce and meat, and hitched up teams of draft horses to old machinery or picked corn by hand to save gas.

The Great Depression was the last heyday of the house-party fiddlers. Once again they were the darlings of the community, magicians who worked their spells to drive away—for an evening, at least—the tribulations of hard times down on the farm.

> With the hard times we couldn't afford to really go too far, you know. Gas—that cost. And we didn't have much money. So we had house parties quite often.
>
> —*Arnold Olson, fiddler*

> One spring we played seven nights straight without a rest. It was in the spring of the year and the farmers were moving. So they were giving each other "farewell dances." They were pretty near all renters, so when things got hard or they got behind on their rent, they had to move. Lots of times they just traded farms. Or left the area.
>
> —*Millard Floyd, fiddler*

With the coming of better times, house parties faded away. Only on rare occasions, like a wedding anniversary or a visit from old neighbors up from a new home in Florida, a spark of music might be ignited, followed by some impromptu farmhouse dancing. But the wintertime house parties—the seasonal cycle of "kitchen sweats"—disappeared from the rural scene.

After World War II, farms became more mechanized.

It was the coming of prosperity. Then you lost your house parties, and barn dances. People had more money now. They would go off to a show, off to some place far away. It broke up your little circle of friends that you associated with.

Your neighbor... maybe you didn't really get to know him anymore, 'cause he went a different way from what you went.

> —*Windy Whitford, fiddler*

FROM NECESSITY TO NOSTALGIA

As house parties were replaced by commercial entertainment, the image of the fiddler changed. Increasingly the fiddler was seen in a nostalgic light, a quaint reminder of a time gone by. One sign of this was the wave of fiddlers' contests which sprang up around the country in the mid-1920s. Ironically, the contests were promoted by the person who brought the automobile to the rural families: auto tycoon Henry Ford.

Motivated by a dislike of black-dominated jazz music and vivacious dances like the Charleston, Ford sought to revive what he viewed as the legacy of pioneer America: the stately, dignified quadrille and old-time fiddle music.[47] In 1924 he sponsored a dance band, the "Early American Dance Orchestra," to make recordings and perform on radio. In 1926, Ford published *Good Morning*, a book of quadrille figures, sheet music, and tips on etiquette and posture.

To broadly encourage old-time music, Ford also initiated a series of regional fiddlers' contests in the mid-1920s, culminating in national competitions. At the local level, similar contests were sponsored by automobile dealers, radio stations, newspapers, theater chains, and service clubs like American Legion and Veterans of the Spanish War. Before the mid-1920s, fiddlers' contests were fairly rare occurrences.[48] But with the support of Ford's highly-publicized campaign, the fiddler gatherings became popular annual events for small towns and larger cities across the Midwest.

That the fiddlers' contests were billed as "old-time" indicates the spirit of nostalgia. The place of the fiddler in rural and small-town life was shifting from the farm neighborhood onto the theater stage. In the footlights, the fiddlers became characters, playing themselves, often in an exaggerated manner. Instead of a role as rural craftsman, the fiddler's image became that of humorous entertainer. At the contests, crowds applauded breakneck hoedowns, trick fiddling (playing behind the back or over the head), comedy routines, and showmanship—or even just sporting an especially picturesque set of whiskers.

If you listened carefully, especially to the older performers, the melodies heard at the fiddlers' contests often echoed of the old ethnic musics of the Midwest, a rich mixture of immigrant traditions. Elder musicians often played community favorites from Irish, Swedish, German, French-Canadian, Norwegian, and other traditions. For elder members of the audience, such familiar house-party tunes would spark a certain delight. For the younger set, though, it was a fading reflection of bygone days. From necessity to nostalgia... the stage was the new dominion of the "old-time" fiddler.

THE STOUGHTON FIDDLERS' CONTEST, 1926-1929

In south-central Wisconsin lies the community of Stoughton, which in the late 1920s was host to a typical small-town fiddlers' contest. Named after a founder from New England, Stoughton was first settled by Yankee immigrants. Beginning in the 1840s, however, there was an influx of settlers from Norway. Attracted by reports of rich farmland in the American Midwest, the numbers of Norwegians on farms and in town steadily swelled, helped by tickets and travel advice

Participants in fiddlers' contest pose in front of local
establishment, Rice Lake, Wisconsin, 1927.

sent back by those who had gone ahead.

The foreign immigrants quickly adapted to styles of farming established by the earlier Yankees, including the cultivation of tobacco. This cash crop helped hard-working Norwegian-American families to pay off debts and improve their farmland. The other immigrant success story in Stoughton was a wagon factory begun in 1865 by Norwegian T.G. Mandt with $100. By 1883 the factory employed 225 men and was selling $350,000 worth of wagons each year. With the wagon works and tobacco warehouses down by the railroad tracks, the community was a thriving community for Yankees and Norwegians alike.

Stoughton was a mix of English and Scandinavian. Christmas was celebrated with plum pudding and roast goose in some neighborhoods, with Norwegian lutefisk and cream pudding in others. Norwegian was spoken as commonly on the streets of town as English. Local theaters offered a mixed fare, from melodramas of the American frontier to concerts of Scandinavian music by Norway's finest, including famous violinist Ole Bull.

The first annual Stoughton Fiddlers' Contest (they would last until the mid-1950s) was sponsored in 1926 by the local American Legion chapter.[49] The event was scheduled for March, a relatively quiet time before spring planting and wagon orders resumed.

Early on a Sunday afternoon, the public thronged into City Hall, where a set of stairs led to a second-floor Opera House. Here was a magnificent theater, 400 seats in the main section and another 200 airy perches in a balcony that rose towards a high, pressed-tin ceiling.

Parents with children in tow flowed down the aisles. Neighbors paused to greet old friends. Musicians carrying battered cases of all shapes and sizes disappeared behind the drawn curtain, painted top-to-bottom with colorful advertisements. Soon the auditorium was filled and buzzing with conversation. Judges took their seats in front and quickly reviewed the categories.

Backstage was bedlam. Musical acquaintances were refreshed with a sip of "fiddler's punch." Contestants scurried about looking for late-arriving accompanists. Some practiced one last time, despite the cacophony of chords, chatter, and tuning instruments. Youngsters playing for their first contest sat nervously on the edges of chairs, clutching fiddle necks hard enough to squeeze a tune out onto the floor, and waited.

Finally a semblance of order was enforced. The mayor welcomed the crowd and took his place with the judges. The curtain was raised and the eager audience applauded the first contestant, a well-versed old codger who wasted no time letting loose with a flurry of rosin dust. The contest was underway.

This small town boasted a wealth of talent. Some of the entrants were outstanding Norwegian musicians who had won prizes in competitions at home in the Old Country before emigrating as young men to America. Their smooth, sweet waltzes tumbled and glittered like mountain waterfalls. Melancholy modes tugged at the heartstrings of compatriots in the audience. Many an eye glistened after a rendition of an old herder's melody or a lively *springdans*. The audience sat and listened "with a sense of reverence," to players like Harald Smedal, Henry Everson, Alex Listug.

Hans Fykerud's music was especially enchanting. A Norwegian immigrant who operated a tavern in Stoughton,

MIX WALTZES AND RAGTIME AT FIDDLERS' CONTEST

A 77-year-old finalist and three of the younger top prize winners of the Old-Time Fiddlers' contest held here Sunday are shown with Ralph R. O'Connor, the master of ceremonies. More than 650 devotees of "fiddle" music heard the preliminaries and finals held at the Madison Community Center. Left to right, those pictured here are Martin Christiansen, Edgerton's 77-year-old fiddler; Theodore Rygh, Jr., Woodford, third prize winner; O'Connor; George Gilbertson, Madison, winner of the $35 first prize, and Herman "Tex" Falkenstein, Madison, second place winner. Cash prizes of $100 went to finalists in Sunday night's event.—(Photo by Kert Bliss)

A mix of old and new.

he had once toured as a concert violinist. With his brother, Lars, the two had performed together in Norway, England, and America. Eventually, Hans settled in Stoughton and his brother returned to Norway. A master of the Norwegian eight-stringed *hardanger* violin, Fykerud was known as a fiddler of mesmerizing power.[50] He could lay a second fiddle on a table and, by playing his own with long bowstrokes, make the second fiddle sing out untouched.

Swede Moseby was another of the local masters. Like some fiddlers, he had a reputation for an affinity for the bottle. One fiddler remembered Swede Moseby's unorthodox version of "Nearer My God to Thee," played as a two-step. But his musical trademark was a flowing, gentle touch with a waltz and many young fiddlers sought to emulate his style.

The Yankees had their favorites, too. One from the nearby community of Cooksville was Jack Robertson. The Stoughton paper, the *Courier-Hub*, summed up Robertson's playing by claiming that he "could do as many things with a violin as a Ford owner with a screwdriver." An old-timer remarked, "that boy could play a fiddle in bed with a quilt over him better than most." An entertainer, Robertson performed crowd-pleasing numbers... with the fiddle held behind his back or under a leg.

To round out the program, the contest offered a range of squeezebox accordionists and hillbilly songsters, ragtime pianists and Swiss yodelers, mandolin strummers and harmonica blowers, ukelele ensembles and Hawaiian guitarists, cloggers and jig dancers.

It was not an easy task to be a judge. The panel was comprised mostly of town officials. One of them remarked it was probably the most difficult challenge of their elected duties.

Dutifully they listened and scribbled notes. As politicians, however, their choices seldom strayed far from the level of applause awarded by the crowd to favorite performers.

At a fiddlers' contest, winning a prize sometimes involved more than just musical talent. A sense of showmanship was valuable. Even a mediocre player who caught the crowd in the right mood and got them clapping in time to the tune might walk off with a prize. Extra attention could be garnered by telling jokes, throwing in fancy bow strokes, or dancing a jig while playing.

One fiddler pretended to be so inebriated that he had to be helped onto the stage by one friend, the fiddle then precariously propped in place by a second assistant. After a few false starts, and a round of snickers from the audience, the fiddler straightened up and ripped off a blazing hoedown—to bring down the house.

Afterwards, the prizes were dealt out, their variety matched only by that of the contestants. The *Courier-Hub* listed the following prize categories for the 1926 contest.

Best All-Around Fiddler
Best Own Selection
Most Different Positions (trick fiddling)
Best-Looking Fiddler
Oldest Fiddler
Funniest Fiddler
Best Girl Fiddler
Youngest Girl Fiddler
Laziest Fiddler
Best "Turkey in the Straw"
Best "Listen to the Mockingbird"
Best Norwegian Selection

Best *"Saeters Jenters Sondag"*
    ("The Herding Girls' Sunday," a Norwegian
    favorite composed by Ole Bull)
Best Left-Handed Fiddler
Best Jig
Best Clog Dance

Like other fiddlers' contests of the time, prizes at the Stoughton contest consisted mostly of merchandise contributed by local businesses. They tended toward the practical—a slab of bacon, a tin of ham, a "good shirt," or "five gallons of the best oil for your car." One fiddler won a window for his house, another got a harness for his horse. Yet another left with a certificate to have his "coat cleaned and hat blocked."

Other prizes bordered on the less practical. One fellow, a non-smoker, won a box of cigars. In the 1928 contest, "Carl Clausen, the mouth organ artist, got a pair of bloomers and a pair of silk stockings as his prize. And Carl is unwed, too," noted the newspaper report.

In case of a tie, the prize had to be divided or shared. This was easier when the prize was a box of chocolates than if a pair of overalls. In the 1927 contest, a pair of overalls was won by not two but three individuals—a tie between brothers Almen and Harry Hammond, and B.L. Bolstad. The newspaper mentioned only the prize, not the solution.

The 1929 contest advertised 75 such prizes. Few fiddlers went home empty-handed. Participants took home an array of hall trees, smoking stands, auto chains, clocks, bags of fruit, and jars of honey. The crowd was estimated at eight hundred, with two hundred more turned away at the door.

Those who did not get into the contest had to bide their time until the dance held that evening at a local hall. Admission to the contest was twenty-five cents; to the dance seventy-five cents. The oldest fiddler that year was Ben Gulhaug, aged 80; the youngest musician was Mr. Arthur Smithback, aged 7, on accordion.

For a young fiddler at his first contest, the thrill came in participating, more than winning a prize. Fiddler Windy Whitford remembered one year being awarded a very large sack of flour for his efforts. A teenager, Windy had arrived at the contest in a Model A, crammed with friends and their musical instruments. On the return trip, they had to lay the sack of flour in the open rumble-seat in back, with two fellows sitting on it. This worked—until halfway home a drenching downpour soaked riders, rumble-seat, and flour sack.

Windy arrived home with a heavy, wet bag, and dragged the sack onto a front porch where it sat for a few days, hardening to a concrete-like consistency. But his mother managed to scrape a few cups of flour out of it.

> And she baked me a cake. She was real proud of me, I could tell.
>
> —*Windy Whitford, fiddler*

Such were the simple pleasures of a Midwestern small-town fiddlers' contest.

"We always wore a Western wardrobe."
—Harv Cox, fiddler

Harv Cox.

ON THE ROAD WITH HARV COX & HIS MONTANA COWBOYS

The fiddlers' contests of the late 1920s were a transition ground where, for a few years, traditions of house-party musicians met with the new sounds of young performers of radio, stage, and recording sessions.

After the applause of the fiddlers' contests, the elder performers went home, and played less and less over the years. The younger ones, meanwhile, were just launching careers as professional musicians. The following interview with Harv Cox outlines a successful career, starting out as a house-party musician and ending up in the early 1930s with his own touring band. The account gives a good overview of changing concerns—from the coziness of "kitchen sweats" to life on the road as a cowboy band.

PM: Could you tell me about your background?

HC: Let's see. I was born in Neillsville, Wisconsin, a "jack-pine savage," in 1906. My Grandfather Moffat played fiddle, and he was half Indian. I played with him a little bit, when I was—you might say—a kid. He had a bull fiddle [bass fiddle] and I got to play on that. I had to stand on a chair to reach the thing.

That was "way back when." Played for house parties... used to call them "kitchen sweats" in the old days. Kitchen sweats—dance right in the kitchen! They'd move the furniture out and dance in two rooms, and the musicians played music [in the doorway] right between the rooms.

PM: How did you start to play fiddle?

HC: It was down in Beloit. I was playing guitar with an old-time fiddler. I was only twelve years old then. Well... he didn't pay me for playing a dance job one night. The next time we went on a job, he asked me if I'd take a fiddle for that night's playing. I got to playing and I got my brother to pickin' on the guitar, and we played house parties like that.

From there we went and tried out at WCLO in Janesville back in 1930. They hired me and the banjo picker that was with us—Oscar Simonson—and we played every noon on the noon-hour show... and an hour on Saturday night, from 8:00 to 9:00.

In those days the money wasn't too good. I think I got ten dollars a week from the radio station. But we played, I think, usually six dance jobs a week besides. Union scale was six dollars a night, so we got six dollars a night. That was pretty good money back in 1930. That was before your time, way before your time.

PM: How did you get started with your road show?

HC: I got to working with Rube Tronson and his Texas Cowboys. They played out of WLS in Chicago, and they picked me up and I put on shows with them.

And at one point their agent got a bunch of dance jobs booked... then they got a big job in Minneapolis, playing on the radio and playing theaters, so they had to cancel these other jobs and get someone else to play 'em. So I had to put a cowboy band together.

I got a guy by the name of Chip Ames on guitar, Tony Zaber on the accordion, got a bass horn player, and Bill Brunton played drums. And I played fiddle, and bull fiddle, or cello.

We played the big theaters with Rube Tronson, and came back and played them again with my band—

Harv Cox and his Montana Cowboys.

PM: Did you have cowboy outfits?

HC: We always wore a Western wardrobe, yes. I wore cowboy boots and all that stuff since I was twelve years old, wore 'em to school, 'cause my dad always farmed with horses.

We traveled over fifteen different states. Wait a minute—I guess, seventeen, you might say. Minnesota, North and South Dakota, Montana... all the states out west.

Barn dances were popular then, and that's the way we made our money. We went out to Montana in 1933 playing barn dances, and you only had to play one dance a week and you made enough money so that you could make a living. Playing just one dance a week!

We stayed with my cousin out there. We had our own bedrolls, and he had a big house, and I could tell you a lot of things there that I could probably get in trouble for. Like we ate a lot of venison—that was our mainstay. We called it "mule's ear."

PM: What was it like, traveling with a road show?

HC: Well, it was a good thing for a young person to do. But you've got to be young to stand it, because it's rough. We had our own tent, and our own bedrolls. We'd play a barn dance, and we'd take our bedrolls and sleep on the barn floor after the dance was over.

We traveled in a 1929 Buick at one time, and then we had a 1932 "straight-eight" Buick... with big steer horns on it. We all fit in one car. Six people. Three in front and three in back.

At one time we had a big Packard, seated seven

people—that thing would go by everything but the gas station! Eight miles to the gallon, and every forty miles you had to put a quart of oil in it.

You entertain people in a town but when you get away from there, you're on your own. Traveling on the road... you never wanted to have a car all paid for. If you got into trouble—ran into someone—they might put the blame on you and try to tie up your car. But if you had a finance company that had money in it, they'd send out a lawyer so they didn't hold your car, and you went about your business.

PM: How did you do the advance promotion?

HC: I had an advance man. He got 20 per cent of the gross. Most of the barn dances we played, we played 60/40. We'd take sixty per cent of the gross, and whoever owned the barn would get forty per cent. If you got 'em on a 70/30, we took most of the money and they were holding the bag. Yep.

In those days, a hundred dollars a night was quite a lot of money. We'd get a hundred dollars for our share, for one night. And when you're on the road like that ... I used to say, I paid the boys "twenty-two fifty per week." That was twenty-two hamburgers and fifty cents! That's about the way we operated.

PM: How big were the crowds?

HC: Oh, three hundred couples. Sometimes it was five hundred. Lots of times, it was 25 cents for gents and ladies free. Sometimes it would be as high as 35 cents, and ladies would pay 15 cents.

That was in the Depression days. But they had a family pocketbook and the whole family came. And

RUSS   BUCK   CAL   NORAINE   CHUCK   "HARV"   EARL

Traveling out west.

know, and there's something about a bull fiddle. When you play it, you probably don't hear it down at the other end of the dance hall—but you feel it. There's a beat there, and you had to go by that.

I played barn dances where they just had kerosene lanterns and no electricity... that was before they even had P.A. systems! One time, after we got going, we got a P.A. system—for A.C. alternating current. And then we went to play in a big pavilion, and we needed power 'cause a lot of people were coming... and it was D.C., direct current! This outfit just didn't work there. So we had to go without amplification, and just "push it out." But I had a loud fiddle....

We have played some flops. But usually there was enough people. We had good billing. And we'd get on radio stations and play for nothing to advertise our dance jobs.

We had picture cards with our picture of the band on it. We put out a hundred of them—the advance man ahead of us. In those days, cowboy music was what people wanted.

I finally quit it when I got myself married and raised a family. Then, I just played occasional dance jobs, and music on weekends.

usually they'd have a place where they could get soft drinks and eat something. And those that drank were drinking bootleg stuff. So that kept expenses down!

We played some big theaters, too. In Chicago. Patio Theater, 8008 Irving Park Boulevard. We played there two days, and we packed that theater for four shows a day, so we made some money there. I think we took a thousand dollars out of there, for two days. And that was quite a lot of money in 1933.

PM: When you played these barn dances, was it hard to make yourself heard with all those people?

HC: Sometimes it was. I played bull fiddle, you

Everett Knudtson, 1981.

Conclusion: The Kingdom of Fiddlers

There is one past but many histories.
—Henry Glassie, folklorist [51]

As I look through my notes, transcriptions of interviews pale in comparison with the images that linger. Thinking back on the fiddlers I met, I am drawn to recall so many small revelations they imparted in their words, actions, or often just expressions that described the nature of this tradition.

There was always something so remarkable about that moment of anticipation when the fiddle was lifted from its case to be tuned... or the twinkle in the eye as a favorite tune was completed and the fiddle rested again in a lap, cradled by strong, gnarled, wrinkled hands.

From each person, I learned something about the spirit of fiddling. As each story was told, there was the invisible presence of many people—spouses, teachers, friends, and neighbors—and a particular place where it all happened.

I remember standing with musicians Windy Whitford and Milo Hoveland in a country garage, playing music and talking about old fiddlers. Windy got a far-off look in his eyes, as he often did—Windy was a philosopher fiddler—and he said, "You know, those old fiddlers... you could close your eyes and pick out who was playing just by the way they sounded."

Then he went on to explain that it was more than just the music. "It was like each of those old fiddlers had his own kingdom... in his mind. When he played a tune, it was all wrapped up in the stories, and the memories, and the friendships that went with that tune. That was his world, that came back to him every time he played." For Windy, the kingdom of a fiddler was a special world of memories, entered through a gateway of tunes with the lock and key of fiddle and bow.

Other more tangible images come to mind. I remember Edwin Johnson, an immigrant Swede, recalling that when he was a boy, he went off with his father to work in a small logging camp. "There were seven men in the camp... and seven fiddles hanging in a row on the wall." I have never forgotten that image. I think by the end of that winter, there were eight—because young Ed made his first fiddle in that camp.

I remember dropping by Orville and Agnes Rundhaug's farmhome for a short visit one afternoon... and ten hours later we were still going strong at midnight, making music and dancing around the kitchen with a roomful of friends who came over for an impromptu house party.

In particular, I remember many trips to try to record old Selmer Halvorsen. He was friendly, but stubbornly resisted my attempts to invite myself over to interview him and record his music. My first phone calls in 1980 were rebuffed; he was busy, or feeling under the weather. I finally just stopped by to see him, unannounced. When he came to the door, I asked, "Are you Selmer Halvorsen?" He gave a great grin, and exclaimed, "I used to be!" We talked for quite a while... through the screen door, which remained closed.

The next visit, we stood and talked through the screen door again, but finally his wife came to the door and invited me in. Selmer did not seem to mind, and his wife, Celeste, was very kind and charming. We sat and talked, and drank coffee. I talked him into getting out his fiddle, and he played, with Celeste chording on the piano. But he declined to be recorded.

Selmer had tremendous pride in his music. His small living room was a fiddler's shrine of sorts, with fiddles hanging in racks on the wall above a small upright piano. Propped up on either side of the piano were two large photos. On the left was 19th-century virtuoso violinist from Norway, Ole Bull, with that name printed on the frame under the picture. On the right, a picture of Selmer, with "Halvorsen" similarly printed on the bottom.

I returned more times over the coming years. Each time I left without a single tune recorded, but with a wonderful time spent talking, looking at photos, sometimes playing music. In 1987, Celeste passed away, leaving Selmer feeling morose. He missed her greatly, and without her chording on the piano, it was hard to get him to play after that... but doing so always seemed to cheer him up.

I can clearly recall my last visit to Selmer on July 14, 1991. Unlatching the screen, he takes my hand and peers steadily into my eyes, his impish face framed by his large ears. He is wearing colorful suspenders which hold up bright blue trousers, and he is in stocking feet. He invites me in and pulls up two chairs by the kitchen table, face to face. We sit and talk awhile about a variety of subjects.

I ask about songs. Yes, he knows some good ones, but no, he cannot sing today; his throat is hoarse. But he tells me about one song sung by the boys from his ancestral province of Solor, Norway, leaving a harbor on a ship bound for America, their girlfriends left behind. Another song, he explains, is a ballad of a boy in the north, who takes a girl away to live on an island. When he comes home one day and finds her in the lap of another fellow, he goes out, grabs an axe, and kills them both. Leaving in his boat, overcome with remorse, he drowns himself. "It's a beautiful song," says Selmer.

After a while, I follow him to the living room, where he chooses a violin and, standing, starts to play. He draws himself up and, in stocking feet, strikes a commanding pose. I am fascinated watching his hand on the fiddle's neck. The thumb sticks straight up in the air, and the other fingers are incredibly large and wrinkled—the hand of a farmer. His tones are sometimes off, but played with conviction, and the phrasing is sharp, syncopated, complex, in a very old style. He is indeed a master fiddler, past his prime but still a great example for a young fiddler.

He tells of a man at a wedding telling him, "Play a good waltz, and I'll give you a good drink." He looks at me. "I did!" And he plays it now, a lively melody.

I throw up my hands. "Selmer, can I record just that one waltz?" He looks at me. "Okay." I dash for the car, bring in the machine, and set it up in a flash. He plays the waltz, then an old Norwegian *springdans*. "How's that?" he says, indicating that is all, and puts away the fiddle on the rack.

On leaving, I thank him for the two tunes and tell him that of the hundred fiddlers I have talked with, he had been the only one who had never let me record. He beams with joy. He is proud of his music. I tell him I will return again to visit... and maybe get him to sing those songs. He smiles broadly—playing has infused him with some elixir.

And recording him—two tunes after eleven years—has done the same for me.

From each fiddler, I learned something valuable. From Selmer, who passed away not many months later, I learned a lot about an old-fashioned way of being a fiddler. Today, most people think of fiddling and music-making as friendly jam sessions, picking and grinning on the back porch with friends. That is true for some, but many of the old fiddlers had an intense pride in their music. They put so much of themselves in the music that it was theirs. The music could be played in public and appreciated at dances, but the tunes were still so special to them, like old prized family heirlooms, that they were not easily given away to other fiddlers.

The best gift for me was the pleasure of seeing, through elder memories, the images of a youngster walking up to a farmhouse in the twilight and hearing music streaming from an open door... the steady rhythm of banjo and piano behind a fiddler's waltz, echoed by the tromp of dancing feet... hours upon hours of music passing through the fiddler's hands... the rising sun striking the frosty panes of a kitchen window in the rosy dawn... the sharp crunch of snow as a path was followed home across fields in the morning, instrument case jauntily slung over a tired, satisfied shoulder.

As fiddler Windy Whitford said of his grandfather... it was as if the old man and the young child had lived through the same times, because they shared between them the same tunes, and songs, and stories.

My role is to pass these stories on to you. These are simple tellings of many people's lives that intersected in music and rural folkways. I hope this book will encourage others to take an active role in helping to recognize and preserve this "house party" heritage.

It is true, homemade fiddling and neighborhood socializing have seen a serious decline since the early decades of this century. There will probably never again be so many fiddlers in the country neighborhoods, playing for weekly dance parties. Compared to an era before radio and cars, before television, movies, and videos, homemade music may never return to its old role in rural life.

But house-party music can find a new niche as a consciously protected and practiced tradition. Earlier in this book, a quote from Windy Whitford may have touched on the essence of a solution. He recalled the difference between commercial entertainment and the old homegrown fiddlers being that of "going to the store to buy a loaf of bread, or your mother or a neighbor baked a loaf of homemade bread."

Perhaps old-time music has the same role in modern society as homemade bread. Most families will consume only mass-produced bread and commercial entertainment because it is so easy to obtain without any advance planning or practice—despite nutritional and cultural deficiencies.

Ove Bergerson, with son asleep on couch in background.

Yet this should not prevent some of us from deciding, for reasons of family heritage, personal taste, or cultural philosophy, to make our own bread, and to participate in some way in our regional folk culture.

Perhaps this book can help invoke a sense of longing for evenings when neighbors used to get together to dance until dawn. Like the smell of homemade fresh bread, this spirit of camaraderie really needs to be experienced to be appreciated.

In teaching about the natural environment, educators describe a biological community as being like a spider's web. Each connection between participants in this network of life strengthens the web. Removing some of the strands weakens the web, although it may not collapse until a certain number of connections are destroyed. It just becomes more and more fragile, until suddenly it breaks and is gone.

Similarly, a cultural setting—such as a rural neighborhood—is like a spider's web. If strand after strand is damaged or lost, one day the web disappears, as did many traditions of rural fiddling and neighboring.

If this is alarming, remember that the opposite is true. A strong web is built strand by strand, too. As each strand is spun, at first it seems so flimsy as to float in space. Then another and another is added, and joined together. By persistence is created something strong, functional... even a thing of grace and beauty.

Perhaps a revival of old-time music is one strand of something greater we are slowly putting back together.

How do we go about it? A final suggestion comes from one of Wisconsin's great conservationists:

On the porch.

Examine each question in terms of what is ethically and esthetically right, as well as what is economically expedient. A thing is right when it tends to preserve the integrity, stability and beauty of the... community. It is wrong when it tends otherwise.[52]

Aldo Leopold was talking about communities of native plants and animals. He probably would have enjoyed a good house party.

Philip Martin
June, 1994

111

Windy Whitford, at home.

NOTES CITED IN THE TEXT

Notes are provided to credit material drawn directly from published sources. Otherwise, all quotes not footnoted, but credited in the text to individuals, are drawn from original research by the author; for a list of fieldwork interviews, see Appendix : Interview Sources.

The Ways of the Fiddler

1. "At this dance I heard...." This delightful description of the fictional character, old Daddy Fairbanks, with his "queer" calls and "York State" accent is from the autobiographical novel by Hamlin Garland, *A Son of the Middle Border* (New York: Macmillan Co., 1936; first published 1917), pp. 79-80.

2. "God bless the man...." From a brief article in the *Stoughton Courier-Hub* (Wis.), Jan. 4, 1907, on early American fiddling, this is a variant of an entry from the humorous lexicon by Ambrose Pierce, *The Devil's Dictionary* (New York: Dover Thrift Edition, 1993; orig. published 1911; portions published 1906): "Fiddle, *n.*, An instrument to tickle human ears by friction of a horse's tail on the entrails of a cat."

3. "He could neither kill a bear...," *A Son of the Middle Border*, p. 27.

4. "This was the best part of David...," *ibid*, p. 54.

5. "Pa had tuned his fiddle...." Laura Ingalls Wilder, *On the Banks of Plum Creek* (New York: Harper Trophy, 1971; orig. published 1937), p. 88. This autobiographical novel from the "Little House" series is set near Walnut Grove, Minnesota, where the Ingalls family moved in 1873. The fiddling of Laura's "Pa," Charles Philip Ingalls, is a frequent wintertime activity in this book and throughout the series.

6. "All day the storm lasted...," *ibid*, p. 294.

7. "When a new-comer arrived...," Col. Daniel M. Parkinson, "Pioneer Life in Wisconsin," from *Collections of State Historical Society of Wisconsin*, Vol. II, Appendix No. 9, 1856, p. 327-328. The passage describes early settlement in Sangamon Co., Illinois, c. 1820, before Parkinson's move to Wisconsin.

8. "I remember once we had a gathering...," from the reminiscences of a an early settler in *A History of Crawford and Richland Counties, Wisconsin* (Springfield, Ill.: Union Publishing Co., 1884), p. 876. Passage quoted by Lillian Krueger in "Social Life in Wisconsin," *Wisconsin Magazine of History*, Vol. 22 (1938-39), p. 166.

9. "... the contribution of a few ounces of tea...," Ira B. Brunson, "Early Times in the Old Northwest," Wisconsin Historical Society *Proceedings*, 1904, p. 165. Passage quoted by Krueger, "Social Life in Wisconsin" (see prev. note).

10. "... dancing over canals," quoted in Harry Ellsworth Cole, *Stagecoach and Tavern Tales of the Old Northwest*, Louise Phelps Kellogg, ed. (Cleveland: Arthur H. Clark Co., 1930), p. 258.

11. "... the taller persons...," *ibid*, p. 257-258.

12. "The good people of the country...," from *Growing Up with Southern Illinois: 1820 to 1861*, the memoirs of Daniel Harmon Brush, edited by Milo Milton Quaife (Chicago: The Lakeside Press, R.R. Donnelley & Sons Co., 1944), pp. 108-109. The quoted passage is from 1839.

13. "... received an offer of marriage...," quoted in Cole, *Stagecoach and Tavern Tales*, p. 258.

14. "The room was decorated with the early flowers...," *ibid*, p. 266.

15. "Kicking frolics were in vogue...," from N.N. Hill, Jr., *History of Licking County, Ohio* (Newark: A.A. Graham and Company, 1881), p. 230. This passage is quoted in "Traditional Fiddling in Ohio History," article by Howard Sacks, in companion booklet to LP record *Seems Like Romance to Me: Traditional Fiddle Tunes from Ohio* (Gambier, Ohio: Gambier Folklore Society, 1985), p. 1.

16. This description of a pious Quaker comes from William Cooper Howells, describing his father, in *Recollections of Life in Ohio from 1813 to 1840*, quoted in Howard Sacks, "Traditional Fiddling in Ohio History" (see prev. note), p. 2.

17. For a good overview of music in logging camps, as well as later developments in Upper Midwest traditions, see James P. Leary, "Ethnic Country Music on Superior's South Shore," in *JEMF Quarterly*, Vol. 19, No. 72 (Winter, 1983), pp. 219-230. Also, for musical traditions of logging camps, see Franz Rickaby, *Ballads and Songs of the Shanty-Boy* (Cambridge: Harvard University Press, 1926).

18. "Nils and I were newcomers...." Excerpted from a story told by Ola Johnson of Wisconsin Rapids to Thor Helgeson, who published in 1915 and 1917 two volumes of accounts of Norwegian-American life in central Wisconsin, which in turn were translated and published by Malcolm Rosholt as *From the Indian Land* (Iola, Wis.: Krause Publications, 1985). The stories are outstanding narratives of early pioneer life. The quoted passage is from pp. 269-271.

19. "Papa's violin...," from the writings of Virginia Pierce Bedford (1791-1882); quoted in "The Devil's Box," article by Joseph Wilson in *Masters of the Folk Violin, 1989* (Washington: National Council for the Traditional Arts, 1989), program booklet to accompany a tour with same name; p. 4.

20. This description of an innovative contraption devised by Andy Sharp, 19th-century fiddler from Lawrence County, Ohio, comes from his grandson Arnold Sharp (b. 1914), also a fiddler, who was recorded by the Gambier Folklore Society, Kenyon College, for a documentary LP *Seems Like Romance to Me*. This passage is from biographical notes by Jeff Goehring and Susan Colpetzer in the companion booklet (see Note #15), p. 7.

21. "A lot of old fellows...," from article by Philip Bohlman, "Charlie Bannen: Spinning Tales and Tunes," in *Ocooch Mountain News* (Richland Center, Wisconsin), August 1978, Vol. 4, No. 8, pp. 23-24.

22. For example, in *Gypsy Folk Tales*, by Francis Hindes Groome (London: Herbert Jenkins, 1963, orig. published 1899), an eastern European Gypsy legend credits the Devil with helping a young girl to win a rich huntsman by fashioning a magical violin—turning the girl's four brothers into strings, her father into the fiddle, and her mother into a bow. The enchanted instrument entices the huntsman, the devil carries them both off, and the fiddle remains lying on the ground in the forest, where "... a poor Gypsy came by and saw it. He played, and as he played in thorp and town they laughed and wept just as he chose."

Variants of enchanted-fiddle legends range from Hungary to Ireland.

23. Across Sweden and Norway are found variants of legends about a musical spirit (in Sweden, *näcken*; in Norway, *fossegrimen*), said to reside in waterfalls, who would teach fiddlers to play or provide magical instruments in return for offerings such as black cats or hamhocks tossed into the water. See Jan Ling, *Svenska Folkmusik*, 1964, or Bengt af Klintberg, ed., *Svenska folksägner*, 1977, for Swedish versions.

24. Various charms were said to be used by musicians in Sweden to ward off rivals, causing strings to break from a fiddle or flies to go up into a clarinet (see prev. note for books on Swedish folk-music legends). Frog or toad bones, produced by burial in an ant-hill, appear in European folklore with a variety of powers, from taming horses to inducing invisibility.

25. In *The Romance of the Fiddle*, by E. van der Straeten (New York: Benjamin Blom, Inc, 1931; reissue of 1911 London edition), the author quotes a 1658 ordinance in Puritan England: "And be it further enacted, that if any person or persons, commonly called fiddlers or minstrels, shall at any time after the said first of July (1657) be taken playing, fiddling, and making Musick in any inn, ale-house, or tavern... or entreating any person or persons to hear them play... shall be adjudged... and declared to be *rogues, vagabonds, and sturdy beggars*, and shall be proceed against and punished as [such]," p. 65. Yet the author also notes that at weddings, Christmas, and Whitsun, the fiddlers were much in demand, despite Puritan animosity to their music.

For a good summary of 19th-century opposition in Norway to the fiddle, see LeRoy Larson, "Scandinavian-American Folk Dance Music of the Norwegians in Minnesota," Ph.D. thesis (unpublished), University of Minnesota, 1975.

26. "For such dereliction...," from R. Carlyle Buley, *The Old Northwest, Pioneer Period 1815-1840*, Vol. 1 (Indianapolis: Indiana Historical Society, 1950), p. 327. Passage quoted in "Traditional Fiddling in Ohio History," (see Note #15 above), p. 2

27. "... there were, then as now, some church ministers...," from the writings of Virginia Pierce Bedford (1791-1882); quoted in "The Devil's Box," Joseph Wilson (see Note #19 above), p. 4.

28. "The young people got around the ban...," from a short article on

social life of Swedish-American community in western Wisconsin in early 1900s, by Oscar Weberg (b. 1891), in *Pierce County's Heritage: Vol. 8* (River Falls, Wis.: Pierce Co. Historical Assn., 1986), p. 38.

29. This story from Westby, Wisconsin, from an interview by the author with Manda Mortenson, is found in the booklet *Across the Fields*, companion to the documentary LP *Across the Fields*, 1982, released by Folklore Village Farm, Dodgeville, Wis. (now available as cassette from Wisconsin Folk Museum, Mt. Horeb, Wis.; booklet is currently out-of-print), p. 27.

30. The eight-stringed *hardanger* violin is a Norwegian folk instrument much like a regular fiddle, with a few noticeable differences. The fingerboard is often decorated with mother-of-pearl and ivory, and the top of the fiddle, instead of a scroll, is a stylized lion's head with a crown. The greatest difference in the music comes from four extra strings which run underneath the fingerboard and through the middle of the bridge. These drone strings vibrate in sympathy with the melody being played and give the traditional music of the fiddle a hypnotic, textured quality.

In the early 1900s there was an association of *hardanger* fiddle players, the Hardanger Violinist Association of America, centered in the Upper Midwest, which held annual gatherings to play, dance, and compete for medals. There is a modern reincarnation of that association, with a quarterly newsletter, *The Soundpost*, Hardanger Fiddle Assn. of America, 2745 Winnetka Ave. N, Suite 211, Minneapolis MN 55427.

Roll Up the Rug

31. This sequence of quotes was assembled by the author, and includes material from interviews with Harv Cox, Bill Brager, Gust Erdman, Vern Laack, Windy Whitford, Ellen Rice Sundin (letter), and Millie Kammerude.

32. This diary excerpt was quoted in Gustave W. Buchen, *Historic Sheboygan County*, copyright 1944 by Buchen, republished (no date) by Sheboygan County [Wis.] Historical Society, pp. 141-2.

33. "Nobody had any money...," from an interview with Glen Westphal, dance caller, from eastern Michigan, published in an excellent book-

let, *House Party: Reminiscences by Traditional Musicians and Square Dance Callers in Michigan's Thumb Area*, Stephen R. William, ed. (Port Huron, Mich.: Museum of Arts and History, 1984, 2nd printing), p. 4. The 68-pp. booklet is currently out of print.

34. See Note #24; this sequence of quotes includes material from interviews with Orlando & Hazel Olson, Windy Whitford, Jane Farwell, Morris Christiansen, Arnold Olson, Selmer Torger, Orville & Agnes Rundhaug, and Reynold Williams.

35. "You are my sunshine...." This story told by Harlan Lee, Brooton, Minnesota, comes from LeRoy Larson, "Scandinavian-American Folk Dance Music of the Norwegians in Minnesota," (see Note #25).

36. This description of the "Jerusalem Fiddle" used at shivarees comes from a book on pioneer life, *Illinois in the Fifties: A Decade of Development 1851-1860*, by Charles Beneulyn Johnson (Champaign, Ill.: Flanigan-Pearson Co., 1918).

37. "Shivaree, we called it." This is from a published interview with Ralph Flowers, fiddler, from eastern Michigan, in *House Party: Reminiscences* (see Note #33), p. 10.

38. From the booklet by the author, *Across the Fields*, (see Note #29), p. 31.

Puzzlin' It Out

39. Colin Turnbull, *The Human Cycle* (New York: Simon & Schuster, 1983).

40. "He was 13 when he got...," from an interview by Jerry Kahlert with Agnes Olsen of Wakonda, South Dakota, about her husband Chet Olsen, fiddler and fiddle-maker, published in newsletter *Upper Midwest Folkways*, Vol. 5, No. 1 (Spring-Summer 1991), Jerry Kahlert, ed., Winona, Minn.

An Era of Change

41. "You can't go to town...," from a famous field study by American sociologists Robert and Helen Lynd, *Middletown*, quoted in *American Heritage History of the 20's and 30's*, Ralph K. Andrist, ed. (New York: American Heritage Publishing Co., 1970), see pp. 26-28.

    For a fascinating, detailed look at a Midwestern town in 1924, and especially the changes on traditions of visiting, music-making, and other recreational pursuits wrought by the automobile, movies, and the radio, see Chapter 17, "Inventions Re-making Leisure," pp. 251-271, in Robert S. Lynd and Helen Merrell Lynd, *Middletown: A Study in Modern American Culture* (New York: Harcourt, Brace & World, 1956; orig. published 1924).

42. *American Heritage History of the 20's and 30's*, pp. 26-28.

43. "They used to call it Hell Center...," from article by Dana Strobel, "Tales of Rattlesnake Tom" (interview with Frank Adkins, 88 years old, Boydtown Hollow), in *Kickapoo Pearls*, Vol. 1, No. 2, published by Kickapoo Valley (Wis.) History Project, Kickapoo Valley Assn., 1979.

44. See James F. Evans, *Prairie Farmer and WLS: The Burridge D. Butler Years* (Urbana: University of Illinois Press, 1969), especially Chapter Seven, "Early Radio and the Illinois Farm," pp. 153-175.

45. *Ibid*, especially Chapter Eight, "WLS: The Prairie Farmer Station," and Chapter Nine "Good Times in Hard Times," pp. 176-231.

46. See John Harrison Kolb, *Emerging Rural Communities: Group Relations in Rural Society*, (Madison: University of Wisconsin Press, 1959), for studies which document a decline in rural neighborhood activities from the 1930s on, matching the gradual disappearance of the house parties. For instance, in Dane County, Wisconsin, studies at 10-year intervals showed a decline in the number of identifiable "active" rural neighborhoods from 81 in 1920-21 to 73 in 1930-31, 53 in 1940-41, and 40 by 1950-51.

47. For a brief overview of Ford's role in old-time music sponsorship, see Stephen R. Williams, "House Parties and Shanty Boys: Michigan's Musical Traditions," in *Michigan Folklife Reader*, C. Kurt Dewhurst and Yvonne R. Lockwood, ed. (Lansing: Michigan State University Press, 1987), pp. 227-228. See also Eva O'Neal Twork, *Henry Ford and Benjamin Lovett: The Dancing Billionaire and the Dancing Master* (Detroit: Harlo Press, 1982).

48. See Steve Kirtley, "Fiddle Contests Through the Years," in *Fiddler Magazine* (Summer 1994), pp. 36-37.

49. Most details on the early years of the Stoughton fiddlers' contest came from articles in the *Stoughton Courier-Hub* newspaper appearing in March or April before and after the annual spring event, with additional information from participants Windy Whitford, Emil Simpson, and others.

50. See Note #30. Further information on the traditions of the *hardanger* fiddle in the Upper Midwest was drawn from the Norwegian-produced public television series on traditional music in the American Midwest, *De Som Dro Vest* ("Those Who Went West"), 1986.

51. Henry Glassie, *Passing the Time in Ballymenone: Culture and History of an Ulster Community* (Philadelphia: University of Pennsylvania Press, 1982), p. 650. This richly-textured field study by noted American folklorist Glassie explores the "fragile worlds composed of mortal flesh, of memory and words" found in the folk history of a small community in Ireland.

52. Aldo Leopold, in *A Sand County Almanac* (New York: Oxford University Press, 1949), pp. 224-225.

"Salty" Hougan's fiddle, with call-letters of radio stations on which he played.

INTERVIEW SOURCES

The following is an alphabetical list of musicians and other key people with whom I talked and conducted interviews. These people are the source of most of the information presented in this book.

In general, on a first visit, I held an interview. Some of these interviews I recorded, otherwise I took notes as best I could at the time, usually writing these up in some level of detail afterwards. In many cases, I also returned for any number of follow-up visits. Return visits generally provided more informal times to chat, to review stories told before, and to get feedback on my preliminary ideas about rural fiddling traditions.

A few early interviews are referenced by year only because of some inexact notes taken as this project started. I did not realize at the time the scope of the undertaking this would turn out to be.

In a few cases, the source of the information quoted was a letter; such correspondence is also listed below.

As elsewhere in this book, place names are in Wisconsin unless otherwise noted. The town listed immediately after the name of the person interviewed indicates the area where they resided at the time of the interview.

For further information, contact the author through the publisher, Midwest Traditions.

Interviews, Visits, and Correspondence

Sam Adank, Fountain City. Fiddler, b. 1904. Interview September 22, 1982.

Hillman Anderson, Richland Center. Fiddler. Interview September 21, 1979.

Rose Anderson, Mahtomedi, Minnesota. Her aunt, Mathilda Saterlie (b. 1890), played the fiddle. Brief interview, July 15, 1988.

Omar Austad, Blair. House-party musician (cello), b. 1896. Interview September 28, 1980.

Adolph Bach, Madison. House-party participant, b. 1920, Switzerland, came to Barneveld area as farmer and cheesemaker. Brief interview August 4, 1986.

Tilford Bagstad, Coon Valley. Fiddler. Visit November 4, 1984.

Olav Bakken, Stoughton. Fiddler, b. 1902, Norway, immigrated 1921. Interview January 21, 1980.

Ernest Bekkum, La Crosse. Fiddler, b. 1917, Westby. Interview August 3, 1980.

Bert Benson, Stoughton. Fiddler, b. 1904. Interview and visits, January 5 and October 6, 1980; May 2, 1989.

Bertel Berntsen, Stoughton. Harmonica player, b. 1891, Norway, immigrated 1912. Interview January 6, 1980.

Ove Bergerson, Northfield. Fiddler, b. 1925, Blair. Led family band, "Notes of Norway," with wife Norma playing piano, son Russell on fiddle and bass, and daughter Renee on banjo. Interview and visits, October 9, 1979; September 28, 1980; and November 21, 1981.

Otto Blihovde, Coon Valley. Button-accordion player, b. 1900. Interview and visits, September 20, 1980, and October 22, 1982.

Leroy Blom, Blair. Fiddler, b. 1924. Led family band, "The Scandinavians," with sons Mark and Kevin, daughters Lisa and Kari. Interview and visits October 30, 1979; September 28, 1980; October 31, 1981; August 26, 1984; and May 6, 1986.

Martin Birch, Tripoli. Fiddler, b. 1909. Interview March 31, 1977.

William Birkrem, Deerfield. Fiddler. Interview January 16, 1980.

Bill Brager, Mount Horeb. Fiddler, b. 1925. Father, Amund (b. 1885), was a fiddler. Interview 1980.

Beatrice Brusoe, Rhinelander. Father, Leizime Brusoe (1870-1949), was champion fiddler. Interview July 1, 1979.

Morris & Ornelius Christiansen, Dodgeville. Fiddle player, b. 1890, and guitar player. Interview 1976.

Ray Calkins, Phillips. Fiddler, led "Wisconsin's Lumberjack Band." Interview 1976.

Clyde Cook, Siren. Fiddler and stage entertainer, b. 1899. Won 22 fiddle contests in a row, lost the 23rd... to his father. Interview September 1, 1977.

Harv Cox, Indianford. Fiddler, b. 1906, Neillsville. Led band, "Harv Cox and his Montana Cowboys." Interviews February 28, 1980, and December 9, 1982.

George Croal, Madison. Grandfather, Thomas Croal (1856-1962), was fiddler. Interview March 24, 1985.

Gust Erdman, Hillpoint. Fiddler, b. 1882, Germany, came to U.S. 1884. Interviews August 3, 1976, and October 8, 1978.

Rudy Everson, Richland Center. Guitar player, b. 1901. Father, Henry Everson (1874-1966), was a fiddler. Interviews September 22 and November 18, 1979.

Jane Farwell, Dodgeville. House-party participant, b. 1918. Brief interview June 16, 1982.

Leonard Finseth, Mondovi. Fiddler (1911-1991). Interview and visits 1976; August 31, 1977; November 3, 1978; October 8, 1979; September 26, 1980; and September 19, 1981.

Ruth Zemke Flaker, Wausau. Participant in German music traditions in Wausau area. Interview October 15, 1985.

Millard Floyd, Rib Lake. Fiddler, b. 1901, South Dakota, lived in Iowa in 1930s, later played with Ray Calkins' Lumberjack Band. Father, John (b. 1868), was a fiddler. Interview March 31, 1977.

Orville Fry, Belleville. Fiddler. Brief interview, May 9, 1981.

Elmer & Anna Gald, Viroqua. Fiddler, b. 1896, and house-party participant. Interview May 26, 1980.

George Gilbertsen, Madison. Fiddler, b. 1925, member of "Goose Island Ramblers" band. Interviews February 17 and November 18, 1976.

Otto Gran, La Crosse. Fiddler and accordion player, b. 1892, Norway. Interview June 16, 1976.

Everett Gray, Richland Center. Left-handed fiddler. Interview April 29, 1976.

Ernest Guibord, Reserve. Fiddler, b. 1903. Father and grandfather were fiddlers. Interview and visits, August 10 and 13, 1979; February 20, 1980; and July 12, 1985.

Selmer Halvorsen, Blair. Fiddler, b. 1900. Interview and visits, September 26, 1980; October 9, 1982; July 10, 1985; May 7 and September 15, 1986; and July 14, 1991.

John Hermundstad, Stoughton. Button-accordion player and fiddler (1882-1981), b. Norway, immigrated 1904 to North Dakota. Interviews February 1 and May 12, 1980.

Werner Hilgers, Middleton. House-party musician. Brief interview March 25, 1985.

Otto & Ragna Holten, Menomonie. Fiddler, b. 1890, and hammered-dulcimer player. Interview October 9, 1979.

Helen Smith Holum, Wilson. Accordion player and fiddler, had four brothers who played fiddle. Interview October 8, 1979.

Alvin "Salty" Hougan, Stoughton. Bass player and fiddler, b. 1919, member of original "Goose Island Ramblers." Father Ole played fiddle, mother Betsy played piano for house parties. Interview January 16, 1980.

Milo Hoveland, Stoughton. Fiddler, b. 1912. Interview September 18, 1979.

Rudy Jackson, Blair. Button-accordion player, b. 1902. Father played button accordion. Interview and visits, May 16, 1976; September 27, 1980; January 12, 1981; and May 7, 1986.

Kenneth Jacobsen, Coon Valley. Fiddler, b. 1921. Interviews August 29 and November 3, 1978.

Bernard Johnson, Richland Center. Fiddler, b. 1907. Interview February 19, 1976.

119

Edwin Johnson, Hayward. Fiddler and fiddle-maker (1905-1984), b. Sweden, immigrated to U.S. in 1924. Interview and visits, 1976; March 4 and October 6, 1979; January 31, 1981; October 23, 1982.

Lavern & Mildred Kammerude, Blanchardville. Participants in house-party dances. Interview, July 13, 1988.

Onie Kelley & Florence Chandler, Eau Claire. Mother, Randie Easterson Severson (1877-1959), was a fiddler. Interview July 27, 1982.

Everett Knudtson, Mount Horeb. Fiddler (1916-1986), led band, "Knudtson Farm Hands." Interviews 1976, and November 23, 1979.

Vern Laack, Mauston. Fiddler. Interview December 15, 1975.

Conrad Larson, Cashton. Fiddler, b. 1892. Interview October 29, 1979.

Lawrence & Lloyd LaPlant, Grand Rapids, Minnesota. Fiddler, and guitar player, respectively. Brief interview, August 4, 1985.

Ethel Lerum, Ferryville. Accordion and fiddle player, b. 1916. Father, Fay Allen (b. 1893), was a fiddler. Interviews, June 25 and July 26, 1994.

Alex Listug, Stoughton. Fiddler (1898-1986) b. Norway, immigrated 1904 to U.S. Interview January 18, 1980.

Alfred & Walter Massart, Rosiere. Participants in area Belgian-American music and dance traditions. Interview March 29, 1977.

Sidney Mathistad, Odin, Minnesota. Fiddler. Interview 1976.

Walter & Caroline McNeill, Mineral Point. Participants in house-party dances. Interview January 18, 1986.

Ellen Wrolstad Mears, Marenisco, Michigan. Participant in house-party dances, father was a fiddler. Letter dated May 16, 1994.

Lloyd Melby, Eau Claire. Fiddler and banjo player, b. 1901, Jackson County. Interview October 8, 1979.

Manda Mortenson, Viroqua. House-party musician. Grandfather, Anton Tomten (b. 1855), was a fiddler. Interviews June 11, 1976, and June 24, 1980.

John Mueller, Sheboygan. Accordion player, b. 1893. Interview November 14, 1984.

Leonard Myklebust, DeForest. Participant in house-party dances. Brief interview May 12, 1981.

Haakon Navrestad, Westby. Accordion player, b. 1905, Norway, immigrated to U.S. in 1922. Interview June 24, 1980.

Werner Nottestad, Cashton. Fiddler, b. 1913. Father John and grandfather Ole were fiddlers. Interview June 23, 1980.

Sylvan Nundahl, Viroqua. Fiddler, b. 1924, member of "Melody Ramblers." Interview October 29, 1979.

Konrad Nyen, Belvidere, Illinois. Fiddler, b. 1926, Blair, member of "Nyens Nordic Band," with brother Ray and nephew Kerry. Father Albert and uncles Ole, Oscar, and Helmer all played fiddle. Interviews April 16, 1983, and October 5, 1985.

Emil Oehlke, Colfax. Fiddler, b. 1890, Green Lake. Interview October 7, 1979.

Arnold & Evelyn Olson, Blair. Fiddler (1912-1982), and accordion player, b. 1915. Interview and visits October 30, 1979; September 27, 1980; and January 12, 1981.

Gleeland Olson, Blair. Fiddler and button-accordion player, b. 1922. Interviews October 31, 1979, and September 27, 1980.

Orlando & Hazel Olson, Stoughton. Dance enthusiasts. Interview January 6, 1980.

Selmer Oren, Montello. Fiddler and banjo player, b. 1909, Stoughton. Interview September 24, 1979.

Christian Peterson, Madison. Fiddler, b. Norway. Interview September 17, 1979.

Sverre Quisling, Madison. Dance enthusiast, b. 1902. Father, Andreas (1859-1911), and mother, Dagny (1869-1952), were both fiddlers. Interview and visits June, 1976; February, 1977; and September 17, 1979.

Lois Rindlisbacher, Rice Lake. Father, Otto Rindlisbacher (1895-1975), played fiddle and accordion. Interview October 7, 1979.

Louis Ropson, Luxemburg. Fiddle-maker, b. 1903, Dyckesville. Interview March 29, 1977.

Harry Ross, Arena. Fiddler. Interview 1976.

Lucille Morse Rowan, Tomah. Fiddler, b. 1906. Interview 1976.

Orville & Agnes Rundhaug, Daleyville. Fiddler, b. 1910, and house-party participant. Interview and visits, September 14, 1980; May 13, 1986; and September 25, 1988.

Herman Rusch, Arcadia. Fiddler, b. 1885, had two brothers who were fiddlers. Interview September 27, 1980.

Art Samuelson, Stanley. Fiddler and button-accordion player. Interview November 8, 1985.

Alfred Schaefer, Mequon. Fiddler, b. 1906. Interview February 5, 1988.

Selmer Severson, Sand Creek. Fiddler. Interview October 7, 1979.

Emil Simpson, Janesville. Fiddler, b. 1901, Stoughton. Took lessons from Hans Fykerud. Interview 1980.

Borghild & Bert Skaar, Taylor. Borghild's grandfather, Kjell Halstien Skaar, b. Norway, immigrated to U.S. in 1868, was a fiddler. Bert operated Lakeshore dance pavilion, Hixton. Interview July 10, 1977. Also, letter dated December 5, 1977.

Albon Skrede, Viroqua. Accordion player, b. 1913. Interviews June 24 and July 28, 1980.

James Smith, Hayward. Fiddler and lumberjack, b. 1884. Interview August 10, 1979.

Ed Stendalen, Westby. Button-accordion player, b. 1915. Interview June 23, 1981.

Ellen Rice Sundin, St. Paul, Minnesota. Letter dated April 28, 1982, with excerpts from Rice family history.

Stella and Ralph Teighe, Viroqua. Participants in house-party dances, Stella b. 1898, Ralph b. 1894. Interview May 27, 1980.

John Thayer, Elroy. Fiddler, b. 1898. Interview August 25, 1982.

Hank Thompson, Park Falls. Fiddler, b. 1878. Interview 1976.

Gilbert Tomten, Westby. Fiddler. Interview November 3, 1978.

Selmer Torger, Viroqua. Fiddler, b. 1906. Interviews June 11, 1976, and June 24, 1980.

Jacob Varnes, Ridgeland. Fiddler, b. 1900, Norway, immigrated to Blooming Prairie, Minnesota, 1915. Interview and visits, October 7, 1979; September 24, 1980; and July 11, 1985.

Gene & Mabel Volden, Westby. Participants in house-party dances, Gene b. 1922, Mabel b. 1919, played piano. Interview 1980.

Knut Volden, Viroqua. Fiddler and fiddle-maker, b. 1886. Interview May 26, 1980.

Sam Walker, Eau Claire. Participant in house-party and hall dances, b. 1900, Norway, immigrated to U.S. 1920. Interview November 3, 1978.

Chick Watts, Middleton. Participant in barn dances. Brief interview, March 25, 1985.

K. Wendell "Windy" Whitford, Cottage Grove. Fiddler and guitar player, b. 1913, member of "Goose Island Ramblers." Interview and visits, September 6 and 24, 1979; May 13, 1980; September 4, 1984; August 17, 1986; and October 27, 1988.

Thanks also to Jan Horne and the "De Som Dro Vest" production crew for Norwegian Public Television, also to Bruce Bollerud, Bob Barnard, Jean Clark, Milo Edwards, Claudia Egelhoff, Chet Garthwaite, Kevin Hoeschen, Anna Kassella, David Listug, Eldon Marple, Vern Minor, Ron Poast, Gerald Regan, David Smedal, Reynold Williams, Jeffrey Wrolstad, and Delma Woodburn for assistance in locating fiddlers and other musicians (and their stories) and bringing related material to my attention.

Selmer Oren (b. 1909) plays a hoppwaltz.

PHOTOGRAPHIC CREDITS

A tremendous amount of thanks is due to the photographers—in the case of historical images, often unknown—who took the photographs included in this book, and to individuals and public archives who have kept these cultural images safe and in good condition.

If you have similar snapshots of family or neighborhood music-making activities in scrapbooks, boxes, or bureau drawers at home, consider the long-range community value of donating them to your area or state historical society or other cultural institution with photographic archives.

Format of Photo Credits
Description of scene. Location of scene (if known), date. Photographer (if known); source of photo (collection which lent the image to the Farmhouse Fiddlers Project), with archival reference number in some cases.

Standard Abbreviation
SHSW: State Historical Society of Wisconsin collections.

All place names are in Wisconsin unless otherwise noted.

Photos by Chapter

p. 2   Frontispiece: The "Big Four" (Nyen brothers band), in farmyard (l-r: Ole, Oscar, Helmer, Albert). Lakes Coulee, near Blair, no date. Photo courtesy Raymond Nyen.

p. 5   Leonard Finseth, at home. Near Mondovi, 1980. Photo by Lewis Koch.

p. 6   Fiddler Ove Bergerson, with Leroy Blom, banjo; James Blom, piano; and Verle Austad, bass. Near Blair, c. 1950s. Photo courtesy Ove Bergerson.

Introduction

p. 8   Otto & Ragna Holten, playing fiddle and hammered dulcimer, at home. Menomonie, 1980. Photo by Lewis Koch.

p. 11   Accordion player Ed Stendalen, at home. Westby, 1981. Photo by Lewis Koch.

p. 13   Arnold Olson at home. Near Blair, 1981. Photo by Lewis Koch (from color transparency).

The Ways of the Fiddler

p. 14   John Fernette, Sr., on stairs with homemade fiddle. Prairie du Chien, c. 1940s. Photo by Helene Stratman-Thomas; SHSW neg. WHi(X91)14234.

p. 17   Alex Smith farmstead. Bear Creek, near Lone Rock, c. 1875. SHSW neg. WHi(X3)31581.

p. 17   Fiddler in front of log cabin (man with beard is T.R. McLain, a Civil War veteran), no date. SHSW neg. WHi(X3)28398.

p. 18   Wedding party on farm. Alma, 1898. Photo by Gerhard Gesell; SHSW neg. WHi(G473)174.

p. 20   Barn-raising in German-American community. Near Plain, 1905. Photo courtesy Gustav Erdman.

p. 21   Logging crew in front of camp buildings. Near Crandon (?), c. 1910-1915. Photo by Anderson; SHSW neg. WHi(X3)18376.

p. 22   Loggers (several with fiddles), in bunkhouse at Ole Emerson's lumber camp. Near Cable, c. 1905. SHSW neg. WHi(X3)1407.

p. 23   Cooks and fiddle players in dining room at August Mason's logging camp. Near Brill, c. 1890s. SHSW neg. WHi(X3)1404.

p. 24   Family outdoors, with fiddle player sitting on chair on porch roof. Near Madison, c. 1875. Photo by Andreas Larsen Dahl; Andrew Dahl collection, SHSW neg. WHi(X3)31304.

p. 25 Charley Richardson (1874-1962) plays fiddle, accompanied on pump organ by his wife Hanna. Wyoming Valley, near Dodgeville, no date. Photo courtesy Jinny Trimbell.

p. 27 Fiddler Anton Tomten (on right) and (l-r) Mathinus Oium, "Kler-Per," and Sibjorn Jackson. Near Westby, c. 1915. Photo courtesy Manda Mortenson.

p. 28 Musical memorabilia, at Orville and Agnes Rundhaug's farmhouse, with poster for concert by Anton O. Rundhaug 1873-1922, (Orville's uncle). Near Daleyville, 1980. Photo by Lewis Koch (from color transparency).

p. 29 Selmer Halvorsen with fiddle under arm. Near Blair, no date. Photo courtesy Selmer Halvorsen.

p. 30 Two fiddlers in portrait studio: Helmer (?) Nyen, on left, with unidentified partner. Written on back of photo: "Taken once when going to play a wedding." Near Blair, (?) no date. Photo courtesy Raymond Nyen.

p. 31 Group of people, with musical instruments, by back porch on farm. Near Sheboygan (?), c. 1890s. Ronald Ahrens collection; SHSW neg. WHi(X3)39938.

p. 33 Fiddler Edwin Johnson (right) and partner Hed Jon, in Sweden. Near Rättvik, Dalarna province, c. 1920s. Photo courtesy Nancy Dahlin.

p. 35 Painted devils dance on side of fiddle once owned by Otto Rindlisbacher, tavern owner and collector of musical instruments, Rice Lake. Instrument now at Vesterheim Norwegian-American Museum, Decorah, Iowa. Photo by Lewis Koch (from color transparency).

p. 37 Musicians and others offer a toast at a Polish-American wedding. Near Weyerhauser, c. 1900. Photo courtesy Anna Kassela.

p. 38 Fiddler and barn-builder Gust Erdman, accompanied on guitar by wife. Near Plain, no date. Photo courtesy Gustav Erdman.

p. 39 Fiddler and traveling salesman Isaac Nelson, accompanied on cello by Rudy Jackson. Near Whitehall, 1932. Photo courtesy Rudolph Jackson.

p. 40 Dr. Andreas Quisling, with fiddle. Iowa City, Iowa, c. 1890. Photo courtesy Dr. Sverre Quisling.

p. 41 Fiddler, with family (?), by back porch. Near Black River Falls, c. 1900. Photo by Charles Van Schaick; SHSW neg. WHi (V2) 516.

Roll Up the Rug

p. 42 William Bell (right) with family and friends on sleigh. Steuben, c. 1900. SHSW neg. WHi(X3)12421.

p. 45 View of farm district from Gibraltar Rock. Dane County, 1980. Photo by Lewis Koch (from color transparency).

p. 46 Large group outside farm house, with tables set for meal, no date. Collections of Farmhouse Fiddlers Project.

p. 46 Farm workers pause for refreshments, no date. Collections of Farmhouse Fiddlers Project.

p. 48 Threshing crew. Near Watertown, no date. Collections of Watertown Historical Society.

p. 48 Klumb barn raising. Holy Hill Road, Germantown, 1899. Photo by E.P. Mueller; SHSW neg. WHi(X3)28614.

p. 51 Farmstead in winter. Near Black River Falls, c. 1890s. Photo by Charles Van Schaick; SHSW neg. WHi(X3)24716.

p. 52 Orville Rundhaug (right) and neighbor Milo Swenson, bows poised. Near Daleyville, 1972. Photo courtesy Orville Rundhaug.

p. 54 Children outside house. Near Cross Plains, 1920s. Photo by Matthew Witt; SHSW neg. WHi(X3)49121.

p. 55 Unidentified button-accordion player, with derby and cigar, no date. Collections of Mount Horeb Area Historical Society.

124

p. 56 Ethel Allen Lerum and brother Morris Allen with piano accordions, outside farmhome. Near Ferryville, late 1940s. Photo courtesy Ethel Lerum.

p. 57 Dance on outdoor platform. Near Black River Falls, c. 1900. Photo by Charles Van Schaick; SHSW neg. WHi(V2)1206.

p. 58 Three men outdoors in winter, toasting. Near Cross Plains, c. 1920. Photo by Matthew Witt; SHSW neg. WHi(X3)49106.

p. 59 Bernard Johnson, with fiddle, and Harvey Peckham, with banjo. Near Richland Center, 1924. Photo courtesy Bernard Johnson.

p. 61 House-party musicians (l-r: John Lund, and Halvorsen brothers, Selmer, Melvin, and Elmer), at Halvorsen home. Lakes Coulee, near Blair, c. 1916. Photo courtesy Selmer Halvorsen.

p. 62 Fiddler Fay Allen (kneeling front center) in the fields with neighborhood silo-filling crew. Copper Creek, near Ferryville, no date. Photo courtesy Ethel Lerum.

p. 63 Roy "Red" Nelson sits and plays by lamplight. Edgerton, c. 1930s. Photo courtesy K. Wendell Whitford.

Puzzlin' It Out

p. 64 Bill Birkrem (holding fiddle), with mother and cousin. Near Deerfield, c. 1915. Photo courtesy William Birkrem.

p. 66 Family with instruments, in front yard. Near Mount Vernon (?), Wisconsin, no date. Collections of Mount Horeb Area Historical Society.

p. 67 Mother and infant child with fiddle. Milwaukee area, no date. Photo courtesy Dorothy Bertolas.

p. 69 Gleeland Olson plays button-accordion, with grandson watching. French Creek, near Blair, 1980. Photo by Lewis Koch (from color transparency).

p. 73 Young musicians gather on porch at Halvorsen farm. Lakes Coulee, near Blair, 1929. Photo courtesy Selmer Halvorsen.

p. 74 Bernard Johnson on chair in farmyard, with instruments. Pleasant Valley, near Richland Center, 1922. Photo courtesy Bernard Johnson.

p. 75 A musical Sunday gathering on the Thomas Young farm. Near Stebensville, Stoughton area, 1928. Photo courtesy Bert and Helen Young Benson.

p. 76 Gleeland Olson, at home, with two-row accordion. French Creek, near Blair, 1980. Photo by Lewis Koch.

p. 77 Conrad Larson, at home, with fiddle. Cashton, 1979. Photo by Lewis Koch.

p. 79 Woman baking in kitchen, 1920. SHSW neg. WHi(X3)31044.

p. 79 "Alice at piano," 1899. Photo by Harry E. Dankoler; SHSW neg. WHi(D28)25.

p. 80 Woman with fiddle and friend on steps. Prairie du Chien, no date. SHSW neg. WHi(X3)34382.

p. 80 Randie Easterson Severson, with two brothers, Pete and Cornell Easterson. Near Eleva (?), no date. Photo courtesy Onie S. Kelley.

p. 81 Young musicians at a birthday party. Near Hegg, 1930. Photo courtesy Selmer Halvorsen.

A Time of Change

p. 82 Two men driving through town. Cross Plains, c. 1920. Photo by Matthew Witt; SHSW neg. WHi(X3)49110.

p. 84 Group of young men pose outside building, no date. Collections of Farmhouse Fiddlers Project.

p. 85 Ludwick and Mabel Kleppe, with two children, on running board of car. Near Daleyville, c. 1930. Photo courtesy Orville Rundhaug.

p. 87 Harv Cox and His Montana Cowboys prepare to play for a barn dance, no date. Photo courtesy Harv Cox.

p. 88   Thorstein Skarning's Orchestra, 1938. From Olle i Skratthult Project Collection at Vesterheim Norwegian-American Museum.

p. 90   Group of young men pose with car outside barn. Alma, c. 1920s. Photo by Gerhard Gesell; SHSW neg. WHi(X3)49130.

p. 91   Bill Birkrem at home. Deerfield, 1980. Photo by Lewis Koch (from color transparency).

p. 93   Publicity photo for "The Hoedowners" (l-r) Windy Whitford, Donna Jean Lundeberg, Vern Minor, Mike Morgan (square dance caller). Madison, c. 1950. Photo courtesy of K. Wendell Whitford.

p. 94   Kitchen social, Selmer Halvorsen holding fiddle (standing). Near Blair, c. 1960s (?). Photo courtesy of Selmer Halvorsen.

p. 95   Harvesting corn in field, no date. SHSW neg. WHi(X3)46278.

p. 97   Participants in fiddler's contest pose in front of Rindlisbacher's Pool Hall. Rice Lake, March, 1927. Photo courtesy James P. Leary and *Rice Lake Chronotype*.

p. 99   Newspaper clipping gives winners of fiddlers' contest. Madison, c. 1930s. Courtesy K. Wendell Whitford.

p. 102   "Montana Yodeling Cowboy Harv Cox," large hand-colored portrait, c. 1930. Photo courtesy Harv Cox.

p. 102   Harv Cox at home. Indianford, 1982. Photo by Lewis Koch (from color transparency).

p. 105   Harv Cox and His Montana Cowboys, on the road, c. 1930. Photo courtesy Harv Cox.

Conclusion

p. 106   Everett Knudtson plays fiddle at farmhome of Orville and Agnes Rundhaug. Near Daleyville, 1980. Photo by Lewis Koch.

p. 110   Ove Bergerson, at home, with son Ryan asleep on couch. Near Northfield, 1980. Photo by Lewis Koch.

p. 111   The Rude family on porch (with instruments, l-r: Dolph, Melvin, Haakon, Sordal, and Oscar). Near Westby, 1926. Photo courtesy Roy Rude.

Appendices

p. 112   K. Wendell "Windy" Whitford, at home. Near Cottage Grove, 1979. Photo by Lewis Koch.

p. 117   Fiddle held by Alvin "Salty" Hougan, with call letters of radio stations on which he performed. Stoughton, 1980. Photo by Lewis Koch.

p. 122   Selmer Oren, at home. Stoughton, 1979. Photo by Lewis Koch.

p. 128   Homemade fiddle from the musical instrument collections of Otto Rindlisbacher, on counter at the Buckhorn Tavern. Rice Lake, 1980. Photo by Lewis Koch.

FURTHER RESOURCES

Magazines

These magazines cover the old-time music scene, with up-to-date listings of coming events, reviews of recordings, information on musicians and regional associations, transcriptions of tunes, and more.

Fiddler Magazine. PO Box 125, Los Altos CA 94022. A quarterly magazine on fiddling traditions. Annual subscription currently $14 (Canada & Mexico $18; overseas $20).

The Old-Time Herald. 1812 House Ave., Durham NC 27707. A quarterly magazine on old-time string-band music, published by a non-profit organization. Annual subscription currently $18 (foreign $21; libraries/institutions: $21).

The Devil's Box. Tennessee Folklore Society, 305 Stella Dr., Madison AL 35758. A quarterly newsletter devoted to fiddle traditions. Annual subscription currently $11.

People Networks

Attend old-time music events in your area. You will meet lots of performers and enthusiastic fans willing to share information about people, places, and resources.

Seek out shops which sell and repair folk-music instruments or sell recordings. These small businesses typically post flyers on groups that meet to play music, upcoming events, old-time music instructors, and so on.

Recordings

Most recordings of regional old-time music are produced by individuals and labels committed to helping preserve this heritage. Besides liner notes, some recordings provide companion booklets with detailed information.

Look first at your local music store. If they do not carry regional traditional music... ask them why not!

Also, many recordings are reviewed in the magazines mentioned above.

The American Folklife Center publishes a free annual list of recommended new issues of American traditional folk music. Write: Selected List, American Folklife Center, Library of Congress, Washington DC 20540-8100.

A small list of recommended recordings is given below as a starting point for your collection of Midwestern traditional fiddle music.

American Swedish Institute. 2600 Park Ave., Minneapolis MN 55407. Several recordings of fiddle music, including *Echoes of Sweden* by American Swedish Spelmans Trio (Edwin Johnson & family).

Banjar Records. PO Box 32164, Minneapolis MN 55432. Old-time music with Scandinavian roots, such as *Old-Time Barn Dance* by the Minnesota Scandinavian Ensemble, and *The Hills of Old Wisconsin* by Leonard Finseth.

Marimac Recordings. PO Box 447, Crown Point IN 46307. A leading Midwestern label of old-time music. Excellent recordings from Indiana, Illinois, and elsewhere, such as *Fine as Frog's Hair* by the Ill-Mo Boys, and several cassettes by Indiana fiddler Lotus Dickey.

Minnesota Historical Society Press. 345 Kellogg Blvd. W., St. Paul MN 55102. Several recordings of regional music, including *Norwegian-American Music from Minnesota*, (diverse artists).

Missouri State Old Time Fiddlers Association. PO Box 7423, Columbia MO 65205. Cassettes of Missouri (and Iowa) fiddle music, such as *Ozark Mountain Waltz* by Pete McMahan, *Old Ladies Pickin' Chickens* by Iowa fiddler Dwight Lamb, *Salty River Reel* by Cyril Stennett, and *I'm Old But I'm Awfully Tough* (diverse artists).

Ohio Arts Council. 727 E. Main St., Columbus OH 43210-1796. Music from Ohio, such as *Rats Won't Stay Where There's Music* (Ward Jarvis Family) and *Traditional Music of Central Ohio* (diverse artists).

Lumberjack fiddle.

Ohio fiddlers. Write directly to Clifford Hardesty, 21753 CR 151, West Lafayette OH 43845 (for cassette, *Ohio's Master Fiddler*); or to Kenny Sidle, 275 Darla Dr. NE, Newark OH 43055 (for cassette, *Fiddle Memories*, by this National Heritage Fellow).

Thimbleberry Recordings c/o Postman North. Rt. 1, Box 195, Calumet MI 49913. Finnish-American music from the Upper Peninsula, including *Children of the Finnish Immigrant* (diverse artists) and recordings by the Third Generation.

Wisconsin Folk Museum. 100 S. Second St., Mount Horeb WI 53572. Small series of traditional music cassettes, such as *Midwest Ramblin'* by the Goose Island Ramblers; also *Across the Fields* and *Tunes from the Amerika Trunk* (diverse artists).

Recommended Additional Reading

Howard L. Sacks and Judith Rose Sacks. *Way Up North in Dixie: A Black Family's Claim to the Confederate Anthem*. Washington: Smithsonian Institution Press, 1993. A history of the Snowden Family, a string band from Knox County, Ohio, active from the 1850s into the 1910s.

C. Kurt Dewhurst and Yvonne Lockwood, ed. *Michigan Folklife Reader*. East Lansing: Michigan State University Press, 1987. A number of articles on traditional music, including "Fiddling and Instrumental Folk Music in Michigan," by Paul M. Gifford.

Elaine Lawless, ed. "Fiddling in Missouri." Special double issue of Missouri Folklore Society Journal, Vols. 13-14, 1991-1992. Order c/o Elaine Lawless, English Dept., 107 Tate Hall, University of Missouri, Columbia MO 65211.